Missionary

Yuan Zhiming   Chen Shangyu

 China Soul For Christ Foundation

Missionary

A Historical Study of the Gospel into China

By Yuan Zhiming   Chen Shangyu

Published by China Soul for Christ Foundation
P.O.Box 1600, Rohnert Park, CA 94927, USA
Tel: 1(707)585-9588
Fax: 1(707)585-9581
Email: info@chinasoul.org
Web: www.chinasoul.org

Copyright © 2016 All rights reserved
Book and cover design by Huang Lu

ISBN: 1-931966-64-8
Library of Congress Catalog Card Number: 2016960880

Compliments for
Missionary

"Words cannot express how grateful I am for my friends at China Soul for Christ Foundation. These documentaries are comprehensive and accessible. They tell the story of God's love and commitment to China for generations. I was brought to worshipful tears as I watched. I experienced great conviction and comfort as I came to the fresh realization that while God doesn't need us to do His work in this world, he chooses to use broken down sinners like me, like you. I cannot recommend these documentaries highly enough."

- Tullian Tchividjian
Author and Speaker, Grandson of Billy Graham

"*Missionary* is a panoramic view of God's hand in the Gospel's advance in China. I was moved to tears multiple times. It is informative, encouraging, and inspiring. You will walk away with a renewed appreciation for missionaries and God's heart for the entire world."

- Bret Avlakeotes
TH.M, D.Min, Senior Pastor, Spring Hills Community Church

"We loved...loved...loved *Missionary* and were deeply moved by God's story of His work in China. The documentary portrays challenges of various cultures working together. It is very encouraging for us Westerners to see the fruit of labor and answered prayer over God's time. It encourages us in our faith."

- Charlie and Dorene Gilmer
A Christian couple

CONTENTS

BOOK ONE - KNOCK

- Chapter 1 The Root 12
- Chapter 2 Legend of Saint Thomas 14
- Chapter 3 Nestorian Christianity in the Tang Dynasty 16
- Chapter 4 Erkeunor Arkaim in the Yuan Dynasty 22
- Chapter 5 Catholicism in the Late Ming Dynasty
    - Part A Francis Xavier and Alessandro Valignano 25
- Chapter 6 Catholicism in the Late Ming Dynasty
    - Part B Matteo Ricci and Xu Guangqi 29
- Chapter 7 Christianity in the Early Qing Dynasty
    - Part A Johann Adam Schall von Bell, Ferdinand Verbiest and Emperor Kangxi 36
- Chapter 8 Christianity in the Early Qing Dynasty
    - Part B The Rites Controversy 42

BOOK TWO - PLANT

- Chapter 1 1807 Morrison's Arrival - 1840 Opium War
    Plowing 52
- Chapter 2 1840 Opium War - 1900 Boxer Rebellion
    Seeding 65
- Chapter 3 Post 1900 Boxer Rebellion
    Rooted 83

CONTENTS

BOOK THREE - SHINE

Chapter 1   Modern Education 98
Chapter 2   University System 106
Chapter 3   Cultural Enlightenment 111
Chapter 4   China's World Stage 116
Chapter 5   Opium Ban 118
Chapter 6   Modern Sports 120
Chapter 7   Women's Freedom 122
Chapter 8   Charity and Relief 126
Chapter 9   Medicine and Healthcare 130

NESTORIAN TABLET 142

SOURCES 155

Behold, I stand at the door and knock.
Revelations 3:20.

Book One
KNOCK

Chapter 1
The Root

The human race is a tree, with civilization at its branches. While they grow in all directions, they share a common root.

This is why all civilizations share the dream of finding their roots.

China is no exception. Since the first Chinese emperor and throughout the Xia, Shang, and Zhou Dynasties, there has always been a Taoist tradition of revering heaven, often through elaborate rituals. Even as the Taoist tradition diminished, people would still cry out to the heavens when faced with pain and suffering, revealing an unwavering pursuit of their roots.

The historian Arnold Toynbee viewed history as a dialogue between man and God: Man calls out to God and God responds to man.

Around AD 1, the miracle of the Virgin birth brought Jesus into the world. Through his extraordinary wisdom, sacrificial love, and mighty power, culminating in his resurrection, he confirmed that he was, and is, the Son of God.

His disciples were confident that he was the source of life, long awaited by the Jewish people, sought after by all.

Before his Ascension, Jesus commissioned his disciples to go forth and proclaim the Gospel throughout the planet.

Trials of blood and fire began to engulf the world.

Chapter 2
Legend of Saint Thomas

In the year 64 AD, around 30 years after Jesus' Ascension, Emperor Nero blamed Christians for the Great Fire of Rome. Six years later, Jerusalem was destroyed and the Christians were forced to flee.

One of Jesus' twelve disciples, Saint Thomas, traveled to India, and it is said that he evangelized as far as China.

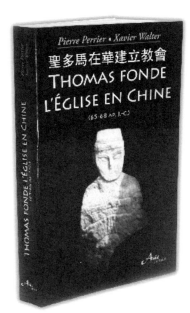

French book
St. Thomas Built the Church in China
by Pierre Perrier and Xavier Walter

In Southwestern India lies the Malabar Coast, and there, in a Syriac Nestorian breviary, it is written: "By S[aint] Thomas the Chinese also with the Ethiopians have turned to truth...... S[aint] Thomas has flown and gone up to the Kingdom of the height among the Chinese."

The Jesuit priest Matteo Ricci strongly believed that Saint Thomas reached China. He wrote in his book, *The Journals of Matteo Ricci*, that St. Thomas is the one who brought Christianity to China.

If this is true, then Christianity may have reached China as early as first century AD during the Han Dynasty. However, we can only consider this a legend as there is little historical evidence to support it. Another legend, that the Nestorian Christian Church entered China in the Tang Dynasty 600 years later, became established as historical fact with the unearthing of a stone tablet in 1625.

Chapter 3
Nestorian Christianity in the Tang Dynasty

In 1625, exactly five years after the Pilgrims landed the Mayflower in North America, also the fifth year of the Ming Emperor Tianqi, the Nestorian Tablet was discovered in the ancient imperial capital of Xi'an.

This precious artifact is extremely well preserved. Today, it can be found in the Stele Forest Museum in Xi'an.

Nestorian Tablet

The tablet's heading mentions the Great Qin. Since the Han Dynasty, the "Great Qin" refers to the Roman Empire. The tablet also mentions "The Luminous Religion," meaning the Nestorian Church. "This ever True and Unchanging Way is mysterious and almost impossible to name. But its exemplary operations are so brilliantly manifested that we make an effort and call it 'The Luminous Religion.'"

After Christianity had become the official religion of the Roman Empire, some believers followed Nestorianism. It argued for the separation of Jesus' divine and human personae, believing that the Virgin Mary should be referred to as "Christ bearer" rather than "God bearer," thereby limiting her role to the mother of Jesus' human form.

Nestorius

The First Council of Ephesus condemned Nestorianism as heretical in 431 AD, so the Nestorians relocated to the East and eventually entered China as "The Luminous Religion."

What may seem, at first glance, to be purely coincidental is: Just as Christianity was traveling east to enter China, the Chinese were journeying west in search of sacred texts.

It is unclear when these legends of sacred texts in the West and the Western Paradise began moving through the hearts of those in the East.

In 629 AD, a Buddhist Monk, Xuanzang, left Chang'an and traveled west to India. Seventeen years later, he returned with 657 Buddhist texts.

However, the Pure Lands in the West that the Amitabha Sutra describes obviously do not refer to India itself. Xuanzang should have kept journeying farther west.

As if it were meant to be, six years after Xuanzang stopped in India in his journey west for sacred texts, Bishop Alopen brought the Bible from the West to Chang'an.

This was the Golden Age of the Tang Dynasty, a time of tolerance and prosperity. Following a personal

Buddhist Monk Xuanzang

*Bishop
Alopen Abraham*

welcome by Chancellor Fang Xuanling, Alopen was granted an audience with Emperor Taizong. The Emperor then arranged for him to enter the Imperial Library and to begin translating the Bible.

Three years later, Emperor Taizong declared that Christianity contained truths beneficial for both individuals and society as a whole and proclaimed that it should be disseminated across the land. He funded the building of a Nestorian church called the "Great Qin Monastery," housing twenty-one priests in the Yining Quarters of Chang'an.

Huaiyu Chen, Cambridge University Spalding Visiting Fellow: In the Mogao Caves of Dunhuang, Sir Aurel Stein discovered a silk painting. Though there is significant deterioration, we can see a person in the painting who is crowned and holding a scepter. On the scepter, there is a cross. On his forehead, there is another cross. It is considered a Nestorian silk painting.

By the time Emperor Dezong ordered the Nestorian tablet to be erected in 781 AD, the Nestorian Church had been active in China for over 140 years.

Text on Nestorian Tablet   *Silk painting in Dunhuang*

Huaiyu Chen: The Nestorian tablet has a section referring to the state of the Church in China, stating that the Tao, or Way, has spread throughout the ten circuits, and monasteries fill hundreds of cities. At the time, the Tang Dynasty used "circuit" as an administrative unit, subdividing all of China into ten circuits. So more precisely, this means that the Nestorian Christians were active in what we would consider economic centers.

Nestorian manuscripts use considerable amount of Buddhist and Taoist terminology. Although these words are simply borrowed, the manuscripts clearly reflect the doctrines and ideals of Nestorian Christianity.

For example, the manuscripts mention the "Great Qin Monastery" which is actually a Nestorian church.

The manuscripts use phrases like "Triune" to refer to the Christian Trinity of the Father, the Son, and the Holy Spirit. "Aloha" is a Syriac term for God. And "Mi-she-he" means Messiah, or Jesus Christ. "Pure Wind" is Divinity, or what we call the Holy Spirit.

The Nestorian Tablet states: "Having designed all things, He then created the first man." It describes precisely the Christian creation narrative.

"A virgin gave birth to the Holy One" clearly refers to Saint Mary giving birth to Jesus.

The manuscript writes "appointing the cross to determine the four cardinal points" to describe the crucifixion of Jesus.

"Ascended to his true station" refers to the Ascension.

"Twenty-seven sacred books have been left." Most people believe that this refers to the twenty-seven books of the New Testament.

With these examples and others, it is apparent that while the fundamentals of Christianity were introduced, there were limits to its influence. Christianity in China still depended on Buddhism and imperial power.

In 845 AD, Emperor Wuzong ordered the persecution of Buddhism, which spread to Nestorian Christianity. Churches were destroyed, priests were banished, and the Nestorian Tablet was buried.

CHAPTER 4
Erkeunor Arkaim in the Yuan Dynasty

The next time the Gospel would come knocking on China's door would be five centuries later, in the Yuan Dynasty. This time, it had to do with the famous Marco Polo.

In the year 1260, Kublai Khan, ruler of the Mongol Empire, met with Marco Polo's father and uncle. Khan expressed an interest in Catholicism and asked them to bring a letter to the Pope, requesting oil from the lamp of the Holy Sepulcher in Jerusalem.

Marco Polo

Kublai Khan

Ten years later, Marco Polo accompanied his father and uncle on their return voyage. They presented Khan with the Pope's response and sacred oil from the Holy Sepulcher. Khan became impressed with Marco. Marco stayed.

Marco Polo lived in China for 17 years. In the widely popular *The Travels of Marco Polo*, the Venetian described the prosperity and grandeur of China as well as Kublai Khan's faith.

He wrote that Kublai Khan regarded Christianity as the truest and best religion, because "it commands nothing that is not full of goodness and holiness."

Christianity in the Yuan Dynasty was essentially comprised of the Nestorian Christians that survived from the Tang Dynasty in Mongol tribes. In Mongolian, they were called "Erkeunor Arkaim," or "believers of God."

Kublai Khan's mother, Sorghaghtani Beki, was one such believer. Some say that there were roughly 30,000 Christians in the capital, making up the bulk of its garrison.

In 1294, China welcomed its first Roman Catholic missionary, John of Montecorvino. This Italian priest opened China to Catholicism.

John of Montecorvino

In a letter to the Pope, he wrote that he had built a church within a stone's throw from the palace, so close that the Khan could hear songs of worship.

Unfortunately, Christianity in the Yuan Dynasty remained limited to royalty and other Mongols and consequently did not spread widely.

In 1362, Zhu Yuanzhang led his Ming armies into Quanzhou, killing the Bishop. Several years later, the Christianity of the Yuan Dynasty was all but extinct.

Chapter 5
Catholicism in the Late Ming Dynasty

Part A
Francis Xavier and Alessandro Valignano

Two hundred years later, at the turn of the 16th century, two major events happened. One was the Reformation led by Martin Luther, resulting in a strong spiritual awakening and renewed focus in spreading the Gospel.

The other event was the successful voyages of global circumnavigation by Ferdinand Magellan and further explorations by Christopher Columbus, connecting the world as one.

Martin Luther

The messengers of God once again embarked on a journey, this time by sea, to knock on China's door.

The Jesuits gathered a group of volunteers willing to lay down their lives for the Gospel. The first to come to China was the Spanish Jesuit missionary, Francis Xavier.

St. Francis Xavier

He stayed in Japan for 27 months.

Fr. George G. Martinson, S.J., Producer Kuangchi Program Service Taiwan: When he was in Japan, he discovered that the Japanese revered the Chinese. The Japanese would often learn and emulate what the Chinese did. Japanese culture had a strong link to Chinese culture.

Fr. Michel Marcil, S.J., Executive Director U.S. Catholic China Bureau: The Japanese, you know what they said? It's strange that you speak of how great Jesus Christ is, but the Chinese have never told us about him. So, Xavier thought to himself, I should go to China. Then Chinese can tell Japanese that there is a Jesus Christ, so that they will believe.

With a strong interest in and respect for Chinese culture, Xavier set sail for China in 1552 and arrived at Shangchuan Island, just eight nautical miles from the mainland, near Taishan, Guangdong.

No one was willing to break the law and take him to the mainland. He died from a fever at the age of 46. Through his last words, he strongly believed that the holy name of Jesus Christ would enter China.

Twenty-six years after Xavier died, another Jesuit missionary, the Italian Alessandro Valignano arrived in Macau.

Alessandro Valignano

Facing China, this large, closed, impenetrable piece of land, he cried out: "O rock, rock, when wilt thou open?"

Even though Valignano was never able to enter China, he was confident that China would be convinced to accept some foreigners of strong intellect and moral standing.

Fr. Georgge G.Martinson, S.J. : At the time, the Jesuits were growing quickly. They sent their best and smartest members to China.

Chapter 6
Catholicism in Late Ming Dynasty

Part B
Matteo Ricci and Xu Guangqi

Four years later, in 1582, Valignano's student Matteo Ricci arrived. Accompanied by his classmate Michele Ruggieri, Ricci

Matteo Ricci

visited the Viceroy of Guangdong and Guangxi in Zhaoqing. The governor of Zhaoqing, Wang Pan, welcomed them and presented them with two plaques for their house and church: "Pure Land from the West" and "Heavenly Flower Temple."

With a strong sense of mission and passion for China, Ricci immersed himself in the ancient Chinese classics while traveling around the country, personally experiencing local customs and culture.

Fr. George G.Martinson, S.J.: Ricci came to China. He believed, "I am a member of the clergy; I should dress and look like Chinese clergy." The religious figures he met were Buddhist monks. For ten years he shaved his head and wore the clothes of Buddhist monks. When he discovered that people really respected scholars instead of monks, he started dressing like a Confucian scholar. He let others know that he was a scholar and started exchanging ideas with other scholars. He soon made many friends among the scholars.

After living like this for 19 years, Ricci finally amassed enough goodwill from the Chinese to become a "foreigner of strong intellect and moral standing." In 1601, Ricci finally received permission to enter Beijing.

Fr. George G.Martinson, S.J.: Unlike other missionaries who tried to impose Christianity on top of Chinese culture, Ricci believed that there were certain seeds within the culture. He wanted to discover elements within Chinese culture that were compatible with the truth of Jesus Christ, and start from there. He felt that the teachings of Confucius and faith in Jesus Christ were compatible and could work together in many areas. The Confucian ethics and values of respecting others and revering the heavens were all acceptable.

He would quote the classic Confucian text, *The Doctrine of the Mean*, "The ceremonies of sacrifices to Heaven and Earth are meant for the service of the Sovereign on High." He believed that the "Sovereign on High" worshipped by the ancient Chinese was God.

On the basis of Ruggieri's *The Veritable Record of the Lord of Heaven*, Ricci wrote *The True Meaning of the Lord of Heaven*. He tried to incorporate Chinese cultural leanings while providing a clear and concise introduction to Catholic theology.

This is another important point. Ricci and others were not only devoted priests, but also distinguished scholars. Ricci brought the eye-opening diorama, chiming clock, sundial, and world map to China.

The True Meaning of the Lord of Heaven by Matteo Ricci

He introduced Western hydraulics, artillery, astronomy, music and perspective drawing to the Chinese.

He wrote and translated dozens of texts to Chinese, covering a wide range of topics, including astronomy, surveying, arithmetic, geometry, Western ethics, culture, and philosophy.

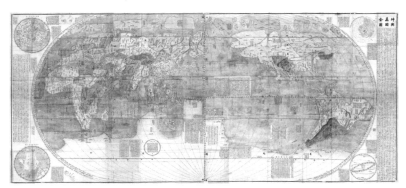
World Map by Matteo Ricci in 1602

Under the influence of missionaries such as Ricci, Lazzaro Cattaneo, and Joao Da Rocha, many Ming Dynasty ministers, including Xu Guangqi, Li Zhizao, Yang Tingyun, were baptized.

Xu Guangqi was the Grand Imperial Secretary. He was the first national leader of China who was both scientifically literate and of the Christian faith.

Xu Guangqi

Fr. George G. Martinson, S.J.: Xu Guangqi was always asking questions and hoping to absorb Western knowledge. Ricci told him: "If you don't understand *Euclid's Elements*, you might not be able to understand Western science and knowledge because Western logic is different from Chinese logic." Xu decided to study *Elements* and helped Ricci translate it into Chinese.

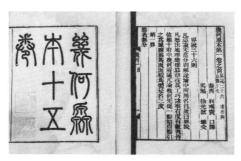

*Euclid's Elements
Chinese translation*

Complete Treatise on Agricultural Administration by Xu Guangqi

He was a farmer and often encountered natural disasters that caused suffering. He wanted to understand how to solve these practical problems. Through the missionaries, he learned and taught people how to grow crops less likely to fail, such as tomatoes and peanuts. He accumulated this type of knowledge for many years and wrote the influential and comprehensive book, *Complete Treatise on Agricultural Administration*. Some say that through this treatise and his many years of research, Xu began a green revolution, increasing the population of China.

Xu and Ricci are inextricably intertwined. If there were no Xu, there probably would be no Ricci, at least not a Ricci with such large contributions. On the other hand, if there were no Ricci, Xu's contributions would probably also be smaller. Ricci should be one of our Catholic Saints. But we also feel that Xu should accompany him as a Saint, because their collaboration is indisputable.

Xu said: "If my countrymen could fear God, serve God, would we not be able to revive the age of the sage emperors?"

Matteo Ricci and Xu Guangqi

In 1616, the Nanjing Church Incident [1] occurred. Allegations were made against the missionaries.

Fr. George G.Martinson, S.J.: Those opposed to the missionaries and unable to accept faith in Jesus spread rumors,

---

[1] The Nanjing Church Incident was the first severe setback of Catholicism in the late Ming Dynasty, initiated by an official surnamed Shen in Nanjing in 1616. Three times, Shen wrote to the emperor, criticizing the creeds and believers of Catholicism, accusing that Catholic activities were associated with the White Lotus Society, a secret sect. As a result, Catholicism was officially denounced. Missionaries were arrested and returned to the South. Churches were destroyed. This incident lasted for three years before Catholicism resumed its activities in 1621 when Shen was dismissed from his post.

accusations, and even formal charges against the missionaries. Every time this happened, Xu Guangqi used his own life as a guarantee. He defended the innocent and good character of the missionaries and offered to be punished alongside them if they were found otherwise.

Together with Ricci, government official Li Zhizao translated two mathematical textbooks into Chinese and edited a multivolume anthology of Jesuit Chinese writings on the fundamentals of Catholicism. Li had concubines. Ricci refused to baptize him until Li finally chose to separate from them at the age of 46.

Li Zhizao *Yang Tingyun*

Imperial Inspector Yang Tingyun was originally Buddhist. After conversion to Christianity, he was criticized by the Buddhist community. He responded: "Christianity is first and foremost the worship of God and secondly the loving of neighbors as oneself. This is completely in line with Confucian teachings."

In the late Ming and early Qing Dynasties, Catholicism and the Chinese government went through a rare honeymoon phase.

Chapter 7
Christianity in the Early Qing Dynasty

Part A
Johann Adam Schall von Bell,
Ferdinand Verbiest
and Emperor Kangxi

During the reign of the Qing Emperor Shunzhi, German missionary Johann Adam Schall von Bell was made the Director of the Imperial Observatory, responsible for reforming the calendar. As a close friend of Emperor Shunzhi, Schall was exempt from court formalities.

Johann Adam Schall von Bell

When the first European style church was completed at Xuanwu Gate in Beijing, Emperor Shunzhi presented it with a plaque inscribed with the words "Spiritual Realm."

Fr. Georgge G. Martinson, S.J: Emperor Shunzhi was very ill with smallpox when he was young. At his deathbed, Shunzhi asked Schall for advice about who should be the next emperor. Schall told him it would be best to select someone who had already survived smallpox and was therefore immune. That Emperor was Kangxi.

Emperor Shunzhi

After Shunzhi died, government official Yang Guangxian led an attack against the missionaries. He claimed that foreigners could not be trusted. It would be better to have poor calendars than to have Westerners in China.

Johann Adam Schall von Bell

At the time, Kangxi was only eight. The Regent Minister Oboi believed the various accusations and imprisoned Schall, Ferdinand Verbiest, and other missionaries. The following year, Schall was sentenced to a brutal death. The other missionaries were beaten and exiled.

Schall was an elderly man

when he was imprisoned. He soon suffered a stroke and was unable to speak. When he was beaten and interrogated, his assistant Verbiest would help answer.

According to Qing records, on April 13th, 1665, a meteor appeared. At 11 in the morning of the 16th, as the death sentence was handed to Kangxi and Grand Empress Dowager Xiaozhuang, an earthquake struck the Forbidden City and darkness fell over Beijing. The government officials were terrified. The Empress Dowager immediately revoked the sentence and released Schall and the others.

Schall passed away at the age of 75 and was buried next to Ricci in Beijing. Their names were written into the *History of Ming* and the *History of Qing*. Their lives belonged to their beloved China.

Tomb of Matteo Ricci

Fr. Michel Marcil, S.J.: Did you know that of the missionaries Jesuits sent to Asia, only one third would be alive after five years? Yes, for Jesuits, if we sent six people over, we knew that only two would remain five years later. The other four would be gone.

The precocious Kangxi took control of the government and summoned both the anti-Christianity official Yang Guangxian and the missionary Verbiest to the observatory to predict various astronomical phenomena. Verbiest was accurate on all accounts, while Yang failed every task. Kangxi immediately installed Verbiest as the new Director of the Imperial Observatory, ordered solemn funeral ceremonies for Schall, exiled Yang, and imprisoned Oboi.

From then on, Kangxi and Verbiest became close friends. Based on Verbiest's memoirs in *History of the Two Tartar Conquerors of China*, whenever Kangxi was unhappy, seeing Verbiest would immediately brighten his mood.

Emperor Kangxi

Poem by Emperor Kangxi

On March 22, 1692, Emperor Kangxi issued an edict listing the contributions of missionaries to China and granted them freedom to evangelize.

Kangxi even made a personal appearance at the Xuanwu Gate Church, presenting them with two plaques bearing his inscriptions of "Revere Heaven" and "True Origin of All Things." He also composed poetry to praise Jesus:

When the work on the cross was finished,
Blood formed a creek;
Grace from the west flowed a thousand yards deep.
Heaven's gate was closed due to the first man's sin;

*The entire path to salvation is through the Son.
I am willing to accept the holy Son of God;
And as I become his son may receive his gift of eternity.*

Fr. Michel Marcil, S.J.: These are the emperor's words. Other documents state, when he writes "heaven," we know what he means. When he writes "heaven," this is not a casual choice of wording. His view of heaven is closer to what we call the Creator of all things, the one true God, right? They didn't use current Chinese Catholic terms back then. They had their own terminology, specific to their time. So they use their own terminology to explain. After that, they would say Okay. You could use the term.

"True Origin of All Things" — you can go analyze those words; they aren't heretical. Any Christian, unless you start nitpicking, then you can nitpick.

At the time, the missionaries translated dozens of classic Western scientific works and helped China fabricate hundreds of cannon.

Emperor Kangxi

Every day, Kangxi would ask Verbiest and two other missionaries, Thomas Pereira and Domingo Fernández Navarrete, to come to the palace and teach for two to three hours, covering topics such as astronomy, geography, music, art, anatomy, and medicine. The classes were never interrupted, even when they left Beijing to visit other palaces.

Pereira and Jean-François Gerbillon helped Emperor Kangxi negotiate China's first peace treaty, The Treaty of Nerchinsk, with Russia's Peter the Great. Emperor Kangxi promised in the name of God to abide by the terms of the treaty.

Twenty-some years after Verbiest died, the honeymoon phase between the Catholic Church and the Qing Dynasty ended. The Catholic Church suffered. The fate of the Qing Dynasty steadily worsened.

Ferdinand Verbiest

CHAPTER 8
Christianity in the Early Qing Dynasty

Part B
The Rites Controversy

From 1645 onwards, the Holy See became concerned with the purity of faith in China, reaffirming time and time again: God cannot be translated as "Shangdi"[2] and must be called "Deus." Churches could not have plaques with inscriptions like "Revere Heaven." Christians could not participate in rites for Confucius or worship ancestors. Classical Chinese texts could not be praised, etc.

Kangxi explained that "Shangdi" is precisely the Christian God. The use of "heaven" was not for the physical heaven. Rites for Confucius and ancestors were not religious in nature, but expressions of respect and obedience and not in conflict with Christianity.

---

[2] Shangdi, "Lord-on-High," also called Di, ancient Chinese deity, was considered the greatest ancestor and deity who controlled victory in battle, harvest, the fate of the capital, and the weather. Shangdi was considered to be the supreme deity during the Shang dynasty (1600–1046 century BCE), but during the Zhou dynasty (1046–256 BCE) he was gradually supplanted by heaven (tian).

Fr. Michel Marcil, S.J.: When you just arrived in China, how much did you understand China? You might not even know how to speak Mandarin. But you would come and say: "You can't burn incense here because it's idolatry. You are baptized. Why do you still worship your ancestors?" Even to the missionaries, some would say: "You're not doing your job properly; you're working for the devil. This is heretical." In Europe, we place flowers on graves. Is this because the person buried there still had a nose that could smell their fragrance?

Bishop Charles-Thomas Maillard De Tournon

The Pope sent the 34 year-old Bishop Charles-Thomas Maillard De Tournon to China, threatening Chinese Christians with excommunication. Kangxi ordered for his immediate expulsion.

The Pope then sent Bishop Carlo Ambrogio Mezzabarba to China. Kangxi met with him thirteen times. When Kangxi finally read papal documents which held no room for compromise, he responded as follows:

"All I can say is, how can we speak to those narrow-minded Westerners about the grand principles of China? From now on, the Westerners may no longer practise their religion in China. It is now banned to avoid further trouble."

Fr. Michel Marcil, S.J.: The tragedy was because of the Catholic Church. It had nothing to do with China. Kangxi was incredibly supportive of Catholicism. In the end, Kangxi had no choice. He could not obey what the Holy See ordered him to do. If others wanted to obey the orders, they had to leave China. Kangxi ordered the Catholics to leave.

Ying Fuk Tsang, Director of The Divinity School Chung Chi College Hong Kong: I think Kangxi's relationship with Christianity was one of mutual respect and admiration. Whether or not the relationship went deeper, whether Kangxi actually became a Christian, I think there was still some distance. While Kangxi accepted different perspectives and religions, he would still place them within Chinese traditions. He maintained stability by not allowing new ideas to challenge China's imperial power and social customs. If others agreed and submitted to his conditions, if they could work with him, then it didn't matter what they believed. If others challenged things, they would shake the foundations of his sovereignty. I think that the controversy of rites was really a breach of an unspoken agreement and mutual understanding.

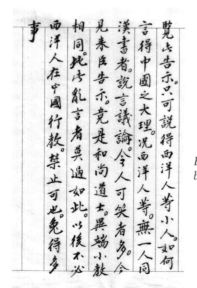

Emperor Kangxi's handwriting banning Catholic practice in China

Emperor Yongzheng

In 1724, four years after Kangxi banned Christianity, Emperor Youngzheng decreed that all Christians were to reject their faith or face capital punishment. All missionaries were given half a year to leave the country.

Over 300,000 Christians were persecuted. 300 churches were seized. Over 50 missionaries either went into hiding or escaped.

Fr. George G. Martinson, S.J.: Whose fault was it? Was the Holy See too arrogant? Or the Emperor too stubborn? Was it the fault of the people, or the will of God? People must decide for themselves. But recently the Holy See decided the Church bore a large responsibility. It was too demanding and not understanding enough of Chinese culture.

If Chinese Christians followed the Holy See, they would not

be able to participate in ancestral rites and Imperial Examinations. They would be considered ungrateful children and inferior citizens. If they followed Kangxi and continued to worship their ancestors, they would have defied Christian doctrine.

At the time, being a good Chinese and a good Christian seemed as incompatible as water and fire.

Under these circumstances, God made the best choices. Especially later. Afterwords, China went through the May Fourth Movement,[3] the Cultural Revolution,[4] Economic Reform and various other assaults. To be a good Chinese today, one no longer has to disobey the Christian faith. Instead, when we need the Christian faith, we can exclaim "God's decisions are always best!"

---

[3] The May Fourth Movement was a student political, cultural, and anti-imperialist movement. It began with a series of demonstrations by students in Beijing on May 4, 1919, in which they objected to what they saw as their government's ineffective response to the Treaty of Versailles. It was an intellectual revolution and sociopolitical reform movement directed toward national independence, emancipation of the individual, and rebuilding society and culture.

[4] The Cultural Revolution, formally the Great Proletarian Cultural Revolution was a sociopolitical movement that took place in the People's Republic of China from 1966 until 1976. It was an upheaval launched by Chinese Communist Party Chairman Mao Zedong to renew the spirit of the Chinese Revolution. Fearing that China would develop along the lines of the Soviet model and concerned about his own place in history, Mao threw China's cities into turmoil in a monumental effort to reverse the historic processes then underway. The movement paralyzed China politically and damaged the country's economy and society to a significant degree. It is considered to be the most severe setback and the heaviest losses suffered by the Party, the country, and the people since the founding of the People's Republic.

Catholic Priest with Chinese youth in Qing Dynasty

From the Nestorian Church in the Tang Dynasty, Erkeunor Arkaim in the Yuan Dynasty, to Catholicism in the late Ming and early Qing Dynasties, spanning over a thousand years; time and time again, knocking, opening, and closing doors; over and over again sowing, sprouting, and removing seeds; all the longing, hoping, and disappointing moments, none of it was in vain. All of it represents God's grace.

Through the missionaries' self-sacrificing devotion to China, we see God's unconditional love for the Chinese people.

From each successive wave of attempts, we see God's determination to be with the Chinese people.

Through each success and failure, we see God meticulously

mapping out a path to the Gospel, one completely tailored for the Chinese people.

In 1807, one hundred years after the Chinese Rites Controversy between the Holy See and the Qing government, Robert Morrison, Hudson Taylor, and many other missionaries, through blood and tears, sowed the seeds of the Gospel at the lowest levels of Chinese society. This time, the door to China's soul was opened. It was never closed again.

THEME SONG
How Could I Not Miss Her

Lyrics by Liu Bannong
Music by Zhao Yuanren

Light clouds drift in the sky,
Gentle breezes blow on earth.
Ah!

The gentle breeze rustles my hair,
How could I not miss her?
The moonlight loves the sea,
The sea loves the moonlight.
Ah!

On this sweet silvery night,
How could I not miss her?
Fallen flowers float on water,
Fish swim slowly under there.
Ah!

My swallow, what did you say?
How could I not miss her?
The withered tree sways in the cold wind,
The wildfire burns at twilight.
Ah!

The west still has some remnants of sunset's hues
How could I not miss her?

*A grain of wheat must fall to the ground and die.
Then it makes many seeds.*
John 12:24

Book Two
PLANT

Chapter 1
1807 Morrison's Arrival - 1840 Opium War[5] Plowing

In 1724, Emperor Yongzheng passed an edict to deport missionaries, closing China's doors and beginning a stagnant time of "peace and prosperity."

Soon after, the Western industrial revolution burst onto the scene, producing textile machines, steam engines, aircraft, electric power, telecommunications, and railroads. Within a few decades, human civilization entered a new era.

Back in isolated China, still relishing in its self-sufficient economy, society was filled with deep-rooted problems, manifesting

---

[5] The Opium Wars were two armed conflicts in China in the mid-19th century between the forces of Western countries and of the Qing Dynasty, which ruled China from 1644 to 1911/12. The first Opium War (1839–42) was fought between China and Britain, and the second Opium War (1856–60), also known as the Arrow War or the Anglo-French War in China, was fought by Britain and France against China. In each case the foreign powers were victorious and gained commercial privileges and legal and territorial concessions in China. The conflicts marked the start of the era of unequal treaties and other inroads on Qing sovereignty that helped weaken and ultimately topple the dynasty in favour of republican China in the early 20th century.

Robert Morrison

themselves through superstition, foot binding, opium, concubines, abandoned babies, imperial examinations, and more.

Facing such an ignorant, vast and distant virgin land, some of the West found it mysterious, some reacted with disdain, and some discovered business opportunities. Christians, however, saw the thirst of four hundred million souls and the call of God's love.

In 1799, as the missionary movement was rapidly expanding in Britain, Robert Morrison was moved by a desire to minister overseas.

Eight years later, in 1807, this shoemaker's son from Newcastle was chosen by the London Missionary Society to become the first Protestant missionary in China.

Christopher Hancock, Robert Morrison Biographer, Oxford University Professor: And so by the time that Morrison was becoming conscious of life, he was affected by this new spirit. There was an awakening of Christianity within England. With that, there was a growing sense of passion to take the Gospel. At the time, travel was beginning to open up, sea travel was becoming easier. Rail travel was just beginning. And Morrison was in one of those great cultural, intellectual, entrepreneurial moments. It was a turning point in British society, much as we see in parts of the world now. That was the moment. Morrison was born into that world.

At the young age of 25, Morrison cried as he left London. He wrote: "I am alone; to go alone; O that I may not be alone; but that the good hand of my God may be upon me, and the angel of his presence go before me."

Lin Chi-Ping, Founder of Cosmic Light, Professor of Chung Yuan Christian University: He was the first one. No one had any experience. He did not have a powerful force supporting him. He just felt that God had called him. He felt very uneasy himself. After he got on the ship, someone sarcastically asked whether he really expected "to make an impression on the idolatry of the great Chinese Empire"? Morrison was taken aback, replying quietly,

"No, I don't." But immediately he followed up with, "But I believe God will."

September in Guangzhou was scorching hot, but Morrison's living conditions were cold as frost.

The Qing Dynasty had closed its doors for 50 years and prohibited Christianity for a full century. Guangzhou was the only port where foreign trade was allowed and the activities of foreigners were limited to a small area just north of the Pearl River called the Thirteen Factories.

The Thirteen Factories

Morrison's first challenge was learning Chinese. At the time, it was illegal for foreigners to learn Chinese. Any Chinese citizen teaching foreigners Chinese would be tried for treason.

Morrison, at high cost, hired a fearless Chinese teacher. This teacher carried poison and was prepared to commit suicide upon discovery in order to avoid being tortured. To protect him, Morrison took lessons at night.

The cost of living and his education in Guangzhou were very high. Morrison lived in a room in the basement of a warehouse, cut down on as many expenses as possible, ate two meals a day, and eventually suffered from severe malnutrition.

He also suffered from loneliness. He sent out 200 letters in one year, only to receive two responses. He said: "I felt about this time somewhat depressed on account of my being quite alone, and without any person whom I could call a friend."

Robert Morrison's letter to his father in 1807

God was his only support. To encourage himself, he wrote in his diary: "Be strong in the Lord, O my soul. Fear not, only believe."

This firm faith gave him tenacious perseverance. Two years later, Morrison could read the *Four Books*, a set of authoritative Confucian classics. He spoke both Mandarin and Cantonese fluently.

In order to reside in China legally, he accepted a translator post with the East India Company, while laboring over a Chinese-English dictionary, and in his spare time, working on a translation of the Bible.

Lin Chi-Ping: Early on, some people misunderstood Robert Morrison, because he was a translator for the East India Company. But the East India Company was engaging in trade with China, which later became the sale of opium, until the late nineteenth century, when opium sales reached problematic levels. So people say: "Look, this first Protestant missionary is basically involved in the imperialist cultural invasion of China, selling opium to China. This terrible East India Company translator. So the evidence is irrefutable." But at the time, the Qing government had closed off China to foreigners unless you were there for business reasons. In other words, unless you were an employee of the East India Company, there was no way to enter Mainland China.

East India Company

Morrison abhorred the smuggling of opium by the East India Company. He wrote: "This is a traffic which is far from being reputable either to the English flag, or the character of Christendom."

During this period, Morrison was faced with desperate loneliness internally and endless trials externally. Together, these forces almost crushed this lone pioneer.

In 1813, things finally started to turn around. Morrison married Mary Morton in Macau. At the same time, another British missionary couple, the Milnes, came to assist him.

In 1814, seven years after his arrival in China, Morrison's first seed finally sprouted through this tough, hard land. On July 16th, Cai Gao, a worker who had been secretly helping with the printing of the Bible, was baptized in Macau, becoming China's first Protestant.

Not long after, Cai Gao's brothers, Cai Xing and Cai San, were also baptized.

In 1815, William Milne took his then-pregnant wife, Rachel, to Malacca and founded the first Chinese magazine, *The Chinese Monthly Magazine.*

In 1818, Morrison and Milne established the Anglo-Chinese College in Malacca, setting a precedent for the dissemination of Western education to China.

Anglo-Chinese College

On November 25th, 1819, Morrison and Milne notified the London Missionary Society that they had completed the translation of all books in the Bible.

The first Chinese Bible

Morrison had spent twelve years and three months translating the Bible. He wrote: "I know that the labours of God's servants in the gloom of a dungeon have illumined succeeding ages, and I am cheered by the hope that my labours in my present confinement will be of some service in the diffusion of divine truth amongst the millions of China."

Christopher Hancock: There was a great fire in Canton in 1820. He saw his Chinese neighbors showing what he saw to be complete disregard for anybody who lived around them. And that inspired him, and this is the good news. To begin to think about ways he could bring in love, into the way the Chinese understood, the Christian faith, and practical love. Very much like will force. Very clear sense of parallel. The Gospel needs to be embodied, not just proclaimed.

In 1820, Morrison and Dr. John Livingstone founded the first public dispensary in China to help the poor. This was a precursor to the Canton Pok Tsai Hospital.

In 1821, the Morrison Chapel was established in Macau. This is China's earliest Protestant Church. It still stands, right next to the Old Protestant Cemetery where the Morrisons are buried.

Christopher Hancock: He preached many sermons which were hugely fascinating. One of the notes you would get out of that is that God loves the world, doesn't just love the church, and He doesn't segregate. He doesn't differentiate between cultures and languages and colors and things. He loves the world. He loves people. And that was one of the great messages that Morrison brought. He said we shouldn't go to China to try to change the culture. We shouldn't go and try to say that we are better than China. We go to love China.

In 1823, Morrison completed the compilation of his dictionary, titled *A Dictionary of the Chinese Language*. This was China's first Chinese-English dictionary, totaling 4,595 pages. Its publication was of monumental importance to Western studies of China.

A Dictionary of the Chinese Language

*China's first
Protestant minister Liang Fa*

In the same year, Morrison ordained China's first Protestant minister, Liang Fa. Liang evangelized for 40 years, enduring imprisonment and torture, all the while remaining loyal to his faith. One of his books, *Good Words to Admonish the Age,* greatly inspired Hong Xiuquan, the leader of the Taiping Rebellion.

Morrison brought many firsts to the Chinese church and Chinese society. Beneath every little accomplishment, however, lay unimaginable sacrifices.

In 1819, half a year before the completion of the Chinese translation of the Bible, Milne's wife, Rachel, after losing two children, also died from illness.

Two years later, Morrison's wife Mary died of cholera. Twenty-nine year-old Mary was pregnant.

Morrison was overcome with grief. He wrote: "I will not say, 'Grieve not.' Oh no! I have shed many tears for Mary. Let us shed many tears of affectionate remembrance, for she was worthy of our love."

Morrison placed his two surviving children under the care of friends and returned back to Guangzhou alone.

Christopher Hancock: In some of the unpublished letters that I read, there is a little hand-written note from Morrison, and he would end with a note of "papa" or "dada" to his children. And you suddenly realize that this man who appears to all the world as incredibly gruff, hard-edged, capable, and single-minded actually had a very soft side.

William Milne

Less than two years later, Morrison's only companion, Milne, suddenly died after continuously overworking, at the age of 37.

Morrison wrote: "Nine years ago, Mr. and Mrs. Milne were received at Macao by me and Mrs. Morrison. Three of the four, all under forty, have been called hence, and have left me alone and disconsolate! But good is the will of the Lord. They all died in the faith and hope of the Gospel; all died at their post...... Happy am I that none of them deserted it!"

During this period, at Morrison's request, many churches

Robert Morrison

prayed for him, asking for God to be gracious to him, to be gracious to the Chinese people, to extend the years of the world's only missionary fluent and proficient in Chinese.

After Milne's death, Morrison continued to evangelize in China for 11 years. On July 30th, 1834, Morrison, who had suffered from chronic headaches, fell ill in Guangzhou. He died the night of August 1st at the age of 52.

Morrison's body was escorted by his eldest son, John Robert Morrison, to Macau, where he was buried beside his wife Mary.

Morrison was in China for 27 years, during the most difficult phase of breaking new ground for the Chinese Protestant Church. In 27 years, only ten Chinese locals were baptized.

One year after Morrison passed away in 1835, his son, John, and Pastor Elijah Bridgman co-wrote a letter reporting that the first Chinese Protestant Church had been established in Guangzhou, with 12 members in total. They were:

Liang Fa, 48, pastor
Qu Ang, 50, assistant to the pastor
Li, 31, wife of the pastor
Liang Jinde, 15, son of the pastor
Liang Yazhan, 11, daughter of the pastor
Liang Yaxin, aide to Liang Fa
Li Xin, 31, brickmaker
Zhou Yasheng, 25, craftsman
Wu Yaqing, 31, printing assistant
Liang Yadao, 28, craftsman
Liu Shuquan, 38, scholar
Zhao Qing, scholar

John Morrison

Chapter 2
1840 Opium War - 1900 Boxer Rebellion Seeding

Six years after Morrison's death, in 1840, the Opium War broke out. Relentless gunfire blew open China's door.

On August 28, 1842, China and the United Kingdom signed the Treaty of Nanking, opening, in addition to Guangzhou, the ports of Xiamen, Fuzhou, Ningbo, and Shanghai to trade. Afterwards, China also signed similar treaties with America and France, including the Treaty of Wanghia, the Treaty of Whampoa, the Treaty of Tientsin, the Convention of Peking, etc.

Every treaty had a provision allowing Western missionaries to enter China through these trading ports. Those entering China around this time included:

Walter Medhurst, the first missionary to reach Shanghai, founder of China's first letterpress magazine, *News From All Lands*.

Walter Medhurst

Samuel Dyer, father-in-law to the renowned missionary, James Hudson Taylor. Dyer created a steel typeface of three thousand Chinese characters, the best of its time.

Samuel Dyer

Elijah Bridgman

Elijah Bridgman, the first American Protestant missionary to China. He translated for Chinese official Lin Zexu and participated in the formulation of the Treaty of Wanghia. In 1854, he set forth to investigate whether the Taiping Heavenly Kingdom was in agreement with Christianity. His answer was "No."

Karl Gützlaff, the first missionary to reach inland China, distinguished scholar, and author of 61 Chinese and 23 English, German, Dutch, and Japanese works. He participated in the formulation of the Treaty of Nanking.

Karl Gützlaff

Samuel Williams

Samuel Williams, missionary, diplomat, and Sinologist. He wrote *The Middle Kingdom*, widely considered a pioneering work in American studies of China. He participated in the formulation of the Treaty of Tientsin.

Peter Parker, the first medical missionary in China. He founded the Canton Ophthalmic Hospital, which later became the Canton Pok Tsai Hospital. He also served as U.S. Ambassador to China.

Peter Parker

Issachar Roberts

Issachar Roberts, who led a congregation of lepers in China. In 1847, leader of the Taiping Heavenly Kingdom Hong Xiuquan requested to be baptized in Roberts' church in Guangzhou. Roberts refused.

James Hudson Taylor

In 1854, James Hudson Taylor came to China, driving the Gospel from the coasts further inland.

At the age of 17, Taylor committed himself to becoming a missionary. After four years of medical and physical training, he left his family at 21, embarking on a 156-day voyage before arriving in Shanghai.

Hudson Taylor's hometown Barnsley

He rented a local residence that served as a clinic, school, and church. Together with other missionaries, he made 18 evangelizing tours in the Jiangsu and Zhejiang provinces, simultaneously providing medical services and preaching.

Mother with Hudson Taylor and his sister

Unlike many other Westerners of the time, Taylor adopted Chinese clothing, ate Chinese food, and even shaved his forehead, leaving only a pigtail. He had no hesitations whatsoever in approaching locals.

Hudson and Maria Taylor

Lin Chi-Ping: This type of behavior brought Taylor a lot of trouble, because at the time, these Western missionaries were British. We know that the British are all about gentlemanship; their culture, their clothing, their appearance – they had a system. Dressing like this is gentlemanly, dressing like that isn't. So when Taylor started wearing Chinese clothes, especially after he shaved his hair and styled his hair in a pigtail, the foreigners could not stand it. They would say, why would a normal person choose to style their hair in a pigtail? We can't stand it! So when Taylor started dating Maria, he ran into some great difficulties. Maria's guardian at the time, Aldersey, who was a really great missionary in her own right, was completely against it.

So we see, Aldersey is clearly a missionary who deeply loved China – she founded a school; she especially focused on education for girls. In China, she had huge contributions, but she was against Maria and Hudson Taylor being together. She felt, her main reason being that Taylor, from her perspective, was forgetting his roots. He was forgetting our British dignity, our British pride, these British things. Later, Taylor would establish provisions that all missionaries that were part of the China Inland Mission would have to wear Chinese clothes and style their hair in pigtails. For this reason, some people left the China Inland Mission.

Taylor said: "It is not their denationalization but their Christianization that we seek. We wish to see Chinese Christians – true Christians, but withal true Chinese in every sense of the word."

This was the time of both the Taiping Rebellion[6] and the Dagger Society,[7] a difficult time of chaotic war and spreading epidemics. In 1858, Taylor lost his first child and his sister-in-law;

---

[6] The Taiping Rebellion was a massive political and religious upheaval in China in the 19th century, sparked by the leadership of Hong Xiuquan. In 1847, he failed the imperial examinations for the third time and was delirious for 30 days. When he recovered, he believed that he and his band of believers had been chosen to conquer China, destroy the demon Manchu rulers, and establish the Taiping Tianguo — the Heavenly Kingdom of Great Harmony. Gathering followers first from the poor and outcast, he and his recruits gradually built up an army and political organization that swept across China. It lasted for some 14 years (1850–64), ravaged 17 provinces, took an estimated 20 million lives, and irrevocably altered the Qing dynasty (1644–1911/12).

[7] The Dagger Society was founded in the 1850s, one of rebel groups either affiliated with or proclaiming support for the Taiping administration. The name refers to daggers used by warriors or martial artists in close combat. The society consisted mainly of natives from Guangdong and Fujian, including Li Shaoqing, Li Xianyun and Pan Yiguo, directors of some of the huiguan or native place associations of Shanghai.

the wife of his colleague, Parker, also died of illness.

From Morrison to Taylor, out of the two hundred-some missionaries who came to China, 40 missionaries and 51 wives died of illness. For a missionary entering inland China at the time, the average life expectancy was only seven years.

In 1860, Taylor's church in Ningbo had 21 people, but he fell ill, was extremely weak, and had to return to England for treatment.

James Hudson Taylor in 1860

Tony Lambert, China Inland Mission historian, former British diplomat to China and Japan: Let's face it, I mean, Hudson Taylor had some pretty difficult times. He had basically, as I understand, what we probably call a nervous breakdown, at one stage. On several occasions his health was very poor. He lost his wife. And then of course there was the terrible shock of, you know, workers he called out on the field dying of disease or different circumstances. So he knew suffering in a very deep level, but through it all, he also knew that the Lord was with him. So I think his faith was very deep, very real.

In England, he would often pull out a Chinese map to pray for places where he had served and also pray for the 11 inland provinces where the Gospel had not yet reached.

China Inland Map

One day in 1865, Taylor was at a large gathering of a thousand people in Brighton. Before his eyes, he saw one joyful British smile after another, while in his heart, he was reflecting on one hungering Chinese face after another. He prayed silently for God to send "24 willing, skillful laborers" to inland China, two for each of the 11 provinces plus Mongolia.

The next day, Taylor opened a bank account for the China Inland Mission in London and deposited ten pounds. He said, this is not simply ten pounds, but "ten pounds and all the promises of God."

In September 1866, the Taylors, with their four young children, along with the 16 other missionaries in the China Inland Mission, arrived in China. They established their headquarters in Hangzhou, at one New Lane.

China Inland Mission first group of missionaries

The following year, Taylor appointed a Chinese pastor, Wang Laijun, to take charge of the church in Hangzhou. Taylor himself led a group of missionaries that set out for the 11 inland provinces.

For the next twenty years, 137 missionaries came to China through the China Inland Mission, establishing 45 churches, 141 mission stations, and baptizing 1,764 people.

At the same time, all major Christian denominations sent people to China. By 1894, 1,324 missionaries had gone to China.

Wang Laijun

Especially noteworthy, seven students from Cambridge University and the Royal Military Academy came to China in 1885, often referred to as the Cambridge Seven. They went deep into places such as Shanxi, Sichuan, Gansu, and Tibet to improve education and spread the Gospel, dedicating their youth to China. They were:

    Charles T. Studd, famous cricketer
    Stanley P. Smith, Trinity College rowing captain
    Dixon Edward Hoste, royal Military Academy student,
        son of a Major General
    Montagu H. P. Beauchamp, son of a Baronet,
        rowing team member
    William W. Cassels, Anglican bishop
    Arthur T. Polhill-Turner and Cecil H. Polhill-Turner,
        brothers, sons of a Captain

Cambridge Seven

By the early 20th century, missionaries had traversed every province in China. They brought not only the Gospel to all the places they went, but also music, culture, education, healthcare, charity, and more. In heaven and on earth, none will forget these sacrificial pioneers.

Although the missionaries did indeed come to China with love, they also did have to enter by means of force, coming in through the openings that had been created by war and international conflicts.

The misunderstandings brought about by suspicion, hostility, and cultural differences eventually caused the Chinese to slowly turn their anger toward the missionaries. Anti-Christian activities began occurring frequently across China, in what were called "missionary incidents."

After the Opium Wars, there were more than 400 missionary incidents of different magnitudes, eventually culminating in the Boxer Rebellion[8] that shocked the world.

In the summer of 1900, within a month and with a slogan

---

[8] The Boxer Rebellion occurred in 1900 when the Society of the Righteous and Harmonious Fists, a Chinese secret organization, led an uprising in northern China against the spread of Western and Japanese influence. The rebels, or Boxers, who performed physical exercises that they believed would make them able to withstand bullets, killed foreigners and Chinese Christians, and destroyed foreign property. From June to August, the Boxers besieged the foreign district of Beijing (then called Peking), China's capital, until an international force subdued the uprising. By the terms of the Boxer Protocol, which officially ended the rebellion in 1901, China agreed to pay more than $330 million in reparations.

Beijing in ruin during Boxer Rebellion

of "support the Qing, destroy the foreigners, demolish the church, and destroy the barbarians," from Shandong and Shanxi to Hunan and Zhejiang, the Boxers massacred 241 Western missionaries and over 30,000 Chinese Christians.

Nearly 10,000 residential homes were burnt in Beijing. The Japanese and German ambassadors to Beijing were assassinated. On June 20, the Empress Dowager Cixi ordered for the attack on embassies in the Legation Quarter. On the 21st, Cixi declared war against all foreign powers.

Next, Japan, the British Empire, the United States, France, Russia, Germany, Austria-Hungary, and Italy formed the Eight-Nation Alliance, and with a combined force of around sixty thousand soldiers, captured Tianjin and occupied Beijing. The Qing government was forced to sign the humiliating Boxer Protocol.

Empress Dowager Cixi

At this brutal time, the Western missionaries behaved starkly different from their governments. They were loyal to the One who had called them to China, the Lord Jesus Christ. They did not hate, did not resist, and did not even complain.

Rev. Carl Lundberg, who was martyred in Inner Mongolia, wrote in one of his last letters: "We do not want to die with weapons in our hands. If God permits they may take our lives."

Martyr Miss Susan Rowena Bird

Martyr Horace Pitkin

Rev. Horace Pitkin, a Yale graduate who was martyred in Baoding, Hebei, wrote a letter to his wife, which he buried beneath the church. In case the letters would not be found, his last words to a servant were: "Tell the mother of little Horace to tell Horace that his father's last wish was that when he is 25 years of age, he should come to China as a missionary."

Before she was martyred, the 28 year-old Annie Eldred wrote in a letter to her family: "I do love the people so, and want to stay with them...... but I will leave it all to [God], and learn to be content, and gladly say, 'Thy will be done.'"

During the missionary incidents, 13 missionaries and five children from Oberlin College were martyred in Shanxi. One of them, Elizabeth Atwater, wrote a letter of farewell to her family:

"I do not regret coming to China, but I am sorry I have done so little...... I send my love to you all, the dear friends who remember me."

Hudson Taylor, Griffith John, William A. P. Martin

During the Boxer Rebellion, 58 missionaries and 21 children from the China Inland Mission were martyred. At the time, Hudson Taylor was in Switzerland recovering from illness, and upon hearing this news, he was stricken with grief and almost inconsolable. He wrote: "I cannot read, I cannot think, I cannot even pray, but I can trust."

According to the terms set forth in the Boxer Protocol, the Qing government was to provide large sums of money as compensation, called indemnities, to the missionaries. Taylor, on behalf of the China Inland Mission, renounced any claims to compensation.

Tony Lambert: Under the treaty arrangements with the Qing Empress Cixi many countries claimed money. Hudson Taylor said no. We are here for Christ, we know the risk. We knew when we came out to China there was a possibility of this happening. We do not want to claim one cent from the Chinese government. So no money was given to the China Inland Mission at all after the Boxer uprising. And I think, God honored that, because it drew a line between the Western imperialist powers, and of course the Gospel which otherwise would have been blurred.

This statement shocked the world and brought forth an even stronger wave of missions. Seven years after the Boxer Rebellion, the number of missionaries in China had increased to 3,833 people.

The third and fourth generations of James Hudson Taylor

In 1905, Taylor passed away in Changsha. He entered China at the age of 21 and served in China for 56 years. Alongside him, his wife and four children lay sleeping in their beloved land. His descendants, generation after generation, through a long chain of life, continue to fulfill one of his promises:

Hudson Taylor

"If I had a thousand pounds, China should have it. If I had a thousand lives, China should have them. No! Not China, but Christ. Can we do too much for Him? Can we do enough for such a precious Saviour?"

Lin Chi-Ping: Taylor's autobiography was published by the

Beijing People's Daily Press, entitled, *To China with Love*. I think this is a wonderful title. "With love" — what is love? Loving life, loving every single person.

To China with Love

Chapter 3
Post 1900 Boxer Rebellion Rooted

Obviously, as long as Christianity still appeared to the Chinese as a foreign religion, there would be no way for it to take root in China. Taylor had said long ago that missionaries should be like scaffolding and dispensed with once the house is complete.

Liang Jialin, President of The Hong Kong Alliance Bible Seminary: The Chinese often say "foreign religion, foreign religion." The use of "foreign religion" as a description already demonstrates that they reject Christianity as a religion from the West. It is not simply just a problem with the source, it is also its appearance, its content, everything Western. And this creates an extremely large cultural barrier, one that they cannot cross, right? So I think, the missionaries were also thinking about how to localize. They were always thinking about these things. They ultimately hoped for the Gospel to take root in China, hoped to cultivate local believers and local evangelists.

In 1907, 100 years after Morrison arrived in China, various Protestant denominations convened in Shanghai for the China Centenary Mission Conference. They reached a consensus that China must build self-governing, self-propagating, self-sufficient local churches; foreigners should gradually remove themselves from the affairs of the Chinese churches.

If the blood of the missionaries were the grains of the church, then only when the grains died could the ground bear multitudes of seeds.

History is no coincidence. Through the blood of the martyred missionaries of 1900, some babies were born, babies who would later become leaders of the local Chinese church. They were: Wang Mingdao, Yang Shaotang, Song Shangjie, Ji Zhiwen, Wathman Nee, and others.

After the Boxer Rebellion, theologian Jia Yuming, evangelist Wang Zai, founder of Bread of Life Christian Church Zhao Shiguang, founder of the Jesus Family Church Jing Dianying, founder of the Chinese for Christ Church Zhao Junying, and many other local evangelists grew into maturity.

Worship songs composed of both Chinese melodies and Chinese lyrics also became widespread.

Lin Chi-Ping: I once came across a song that early home churches in Henan sang, called *Missing You my Fellow Holy Spirit*. The lyrics were really strange: "Missing you, my fellow Holy Spirit, tears are falling down. When you woke up this morning, did you read the Bible, did you pray? Missing you, my fellow Holy Spirit, tears are falling down." It just didn't seem like a hymn or a typical worship song to me, right? Later, I realized, that the Christian symbolism of hymns had stuck in my mind. So I thought that these songs must have "Holy, holy, holy" to be true songs of worship. But then I realized, these songs were being sung in rural Chinese villages, expressing the suffering in their hearts, a feeling of being separated from their brothers and sisters and not being able to greet each other. No wonder they would cry as they were singing. Once I shed myself of my decades of Christian experience and really delved deep in there, I suddenly discovered, wow, it is a completely different feeling. If I sing this, I would cry too. That was really getting inside.

Localization of language, localization of comprehension, and localization of emotions, together like the Yangtze and Yellow Rivers, surged through China, forming a new local climate.

In 1919, under the leadership of Calvin Mateer and Chauncey Goodrich, after 28 years of translation, the Chinese Union Version of the Bible that is still in use today was published.

Union Version Chinese Bible Translation Committee

In 1937, the Second Sino-Japanese War began. One thousand two hundred Western missionaries were held prisoner by the Japanese military in the Weihsien Internment Camp. By 1945, when the Japanese surrendered, there were only 600 left. After 1952, all were evacuated from China.

Lin Chi-Ping: God is in charge of everything. All of history is His story. All of it is His history. It's all God's history. So some things, when they happen in some period, and we try to reason it out, we can't. Because we are very much limited, and God transcends our reason. These things need to be looked back on, we can look back many years later and suddenly realize, this was the underlying reason. The expulsion of missionaries, we can't only look at it from a negative point of view. Because of these events, the Chinese church was also forced to consider questions of localization.

The seeds have already died, leaving behind an abundance of fruit. God let them go, leaving behind the triumph of their lives, their love in full bloom.

The number of Chinese Christians has been growing like a miracle. In 1845, when Morrison died, there were only ten. In 1906, one century after Morrison arrived in China, there were 170,000. Today, two centuries after Morrison's arrival, there are tens of millions of Chinese Christians!

Christianity in China will never be like the shadow that passed through the Tang Dynasty, or the wind that blew through the Ming and Qing Dynasties, because it has become a faith for the Chinese people.

As we welcome the future with confidence, we must not forget the blood that the missionaries shed in the past. In their blood, we see God's eternal love for the Chinese people.

Pioneer Missionaries Entering China's Provinces:

Guangzhou
1807, Robert Morrison
1830, Elijah Coleman Bridgman

Shanghai
1831, Karl Friedrich August Gützlaff
1843, Walter Henry Medhurst

Fujian
1841, David Abeel
1842, William Jones Boone

Hong Kong
1842, Issachar Jacox Roberts
1843, James Legge

Zhejiang
1843, Daniel Jerome MacGowan
1857, James Hudson Taylor

Jiangsu
1845, William Jones Boone
1867, George Duncan

Beijing
1861, William Lockhart
1863, William Alexander Parsons Martin

Shandong
1861, John Livingstone Nevius

1862, Charles Rogers Mills

Hubei
1861, Griffith John
1865, David Hill

Hunan
1863, Josiah Cox
1875, Adam Cochrane Dorward

Taiwan
1865, James Laidlaw Maxwell
1871, George Leslie Mackay

Jilin
1866, Alexander Williamson
1908, Jonathan Goforth

Liaoning
1867, William Chalmers Burns
1882, Dugald Christie

Sichuan
1867, Virgil Chittenden Hart
1868, Alexander Wylie

Heilongjiang
1868, Alexander Williamson
1923, Alice Mildred Cable
       Evangeline Frances French
       Francesca Law French

Hebei
1869, Devello Zelotes Sheffield

Anhui
1869, James Joseph Meadows

Inner Mongolia
1870, James Gilmour

Tianjin
1872, Arthur Henderson Smith

Henan
1875, Henry Taylor
1934, David Howard Adeney

Shanxi
1876, Francis James
1876, Joshua John Turner

Shaanxi
1876, Frederick William Baller
1876, George King

Tibet
1876, James Cameron

Gansu
1877, George F. Easton
1877, George Parker

Guangxi
1877, Edward Fishe

Yunnan
1877, John McCarthy
1887, Samuel Pollard
1908, James Outram Fraser

Guizhou
1877, Charles Henry Judd
1877, James F. Broumton

Jiangxi
1881, Carl Frederick Kupfer

Xinjiang
1906, George W. Hunter

Ningxia
1917, Samuel Marinus Zwemer
1936, Claude Leon Pickens, Jr.

Qinghai
1915, Harry French Ridley
1921, Victor Guy Plymire

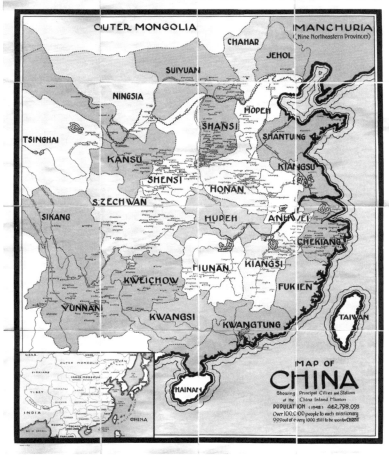

China Inland Mission map in 1948

THEME SONG
Oh, the Sea, Can You Tell Me?

Canaan Hymns #868
Lyrics and music by Xiao Min

The sea, oh the sea,
Can you tell me,
How many missionaries have come to China?

Different languages and skin colors,
But all deeply in love with China.
Enduring misunderstandings,
Dedicating their lives to China.

What did they do this for?
Why did they do this?
Every high mountain,
Every little path,
Has also asked.

They were individual grains of wheat,
Blessing a suffering China,
So that China could have today's harvest,
Mountains and plains filled with fruit.

Oh brothers and sisters,
We must always remember,
They were God's messengers,
Bringing love to China.

Raising high a burning torch of holy fire,
Traveling to every corner.
Next to the deep blue sea,
Who has awakened China?

You are the light of the world.
Matthew 5:14

Book Three
SHINE

"China is a great land and has a great future before it. I am thankful that I have had the opportunity to do what I could to make it what it ought to be."
— Letter to James D. Mooney from Calvin Mateer, Nov 27, 1906

Calvin Mateer

In 1881, the American missionary Calvin Mateer, founder of Tengchow College, which would later become China's first university, lit China's first electric light on campus.

When the sun rises, it does not only shine upon the church. What God's messengers brought to China was the light of the world.

The arrival of Ricci in China brought not only Catholicism, but also science and culture. The arrival of Morrison brought not only the first translated Bible and the establishment of the first Protestant church, but also the first school and first hospital, the compilation of the first Chinese-English dictionary, and the publication of the first Chinese periodical.

The first orphanage, the first school for the deaf and dumb, the first set of Braille characters, the first drug rehabilitation center, the first newspaper, the first experimental lab, the first school for girls, the first sports team, the first participation in the Olympics...... Many of China's firsts were brought about by missionaries. Even the first discovery of the giant panda was by Armand David, a French missionary.

Armand David

It is no exaggeration to say that in every corner of modern China, we can find the dusty footprints of missionaries.

CHAPTER 1
Modern Education

Today, China has nine years of compulsory education and over 2,000 colleges and universities. Every year, around 400,000 students study abroad, more than any other country in the world.

Who would believe that just over 100 years ago, out of the 400 million people living in Qing China, only 40,000 could read, representing a literacy rate lower than 0.01%.[9]

The earliest Chinese school was founded in 1817 by Robert Morrison and William Milne in Malacca. Named Anglo-Chinese College, it began with only three students.

Ten years later, the first Chinese pastor Liang Fa founded the first school in Mainland China with his hometown friend Gu Tianqing.

Another ten years later, Mary Gützlaff, wife of German missionary Karl Gützlaff, and Yale graduate Samuel Robbins Brown founded the Morrison School, the first Western-style school in Macau. In the beginning, there were only six students, including the first group of students to study abroad, Yung Wing, Huang

---

[9] According to Timothy Richard's survey in 1891. Reference: Gu Changsheng. *European Wind and American Rain Swept the Middle Kingdom*. California, U. S. A.: Evergreen Publishing, 2001. P.152.

Samuel Brown   *Yung Wing*

Kuan, and Huang Sheng.

Lin Chi-Ping, Founder of Cosmic Light, Professor of Chung Yuan Christian University: Brown, after teaching for a period of time, his health couldn't bear it anymore and he was returning to the U.S. He asked his students who would be willing to come with him to study in the U.S. At that time, no one was willing to go. Formally learning from "barbarian" teachers was a shame, an indication of forgetting one's roots. Despite this, three students agreed to accompany Brown to the U.S.: the brothers Huang Shung and Huang Kuan, as well as Yung Wing, who we all know about. Following in Brown's footsteps, Yung Wing attended Yale.

Huang Kuan went on to study medicine at the University of Edinburgh and became China's first Western medical doctor. After Yung Wing returned to China, he started an important project to help young Chinese children to study abroad. He felt that it was necessary to have people interact with the West at a young age so that they would truly understand the West. This was building a foundation. Some other important historical figures emerged from

Yung Wing's Chinese Educational Mission.

For example, Zhan Tianyou, "Father of Modern Engineering," was brought out by Yung. Tung Shaoyi, the first Premier of the Republic of China, was also brought out by him. Many important figures in the modernization of China throughout the late Qing and early Republic periods were students that Yung took abroad. It clearly influenced the subsequent trends toward learning from the West, till the Republic, that continues today.

In 1842, before the Second Opium War, the missionaries had established 50 schools in China. Following the Opium Wars and the subsequent Treaty of Nanjing and Convention of Peking, by 1877, there were as many as 347 Christian schools.

In 1877, the first General Conference of the Protestant Missionaries of China was held. They decided to form a committee to prepare a series of schoolbooks. Afterwards, under the leadership of missionaries William Martin, Alexander Williamson, Calvin Mateer, Young Allen, Rudolf Lechler, and John Fryer, 59

Math textbooks by Calvin Mateer

schoolbooks were written and compiled. Around 30,000 copies were published.

Higher education came to China a few centuries later than it came to the West. The ones who finally connected China's higher education system with the rest of the world were also the Western missionaries.

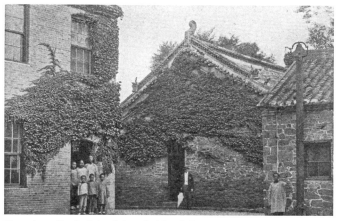

Tengchow Boy's School founded by Calvin Mateer in 1864

Missionary Calvin Mateer founded the Tengchow Boy's School in 1864, recruiting six students from impoverished families and providing them with stationery, clothing, and food. In 1876, the school was renamed Tengchow College, later becoming China's first university.

Another American missionary, Hunter Corbett, founded over 40 schools in Yantai, as well as a hospital and a museum. He was recognized for his work first by the Qing Emperor Guangxu, and later by President Yuan Shikai.

Hunter Corbett

John Fryer

The British missionary John Fryer established China's first science class in 1866, founded China's first polytechnic institution in 1874, and published China's first scientific magazine in 1875. He also translated over 100 scientific works into Chinese.

In Southern China, the earliest university was St. John's University, founded by Samuel Schereschewsky in 1879.

Other early universities in China founded by missionaries include:
1888, Nanking University
1889, North China College
1897, Hangchow Presbyterian College

The early days of every one of these universities were extremely difficult. When Nanking University was first founded, only three boys enrolled. As a reward for their attendance, the university gave them a bowl of rice each day.

Unlike today, where students apply to schools and pay tuition, at that time, the schools would invite students to attend and pay for their living expenses.

The funds to run each school were mostly provided through donations from the missionaries' home churches. Every dollar expressed love from thousands of miles away.

By 1900, on the brink of the Boxer Rebellion, missionaries had established as many as 2,000 primary schools, secondary schools, and colleges.

The Boxer Rebellion was disastrous for the fledgling Chinese educational system; schools around the country suffered from damage and destruction.

But light is unstoppable by darkness. The British missionary Timothy Richard convinced his government to use the indemnity funds paid by the Qing government to establish Shanxi University.

Shanxi University letterhead

American missionary Arthur Smith and others also convinced the American Congress to use their indemnity funds to establish Tsinghua College, the precursor to Tsinghua University.

The other Western countries followed suit, not only using the large sums of indemnity funds to establish schools in China, but also forcing the Chinese government to reform its antiquated Imperial Examination system, establish science and engineering as academic subjects, and open up opportunities for its citizens to study abroad.

Less than 20 years later, according to surveys in 1918, the number of schools founded by missionaries in China had surged from 2,000 before the Boxer Rebellion to a total of 7,382 schools.

Timothy Richard

Li Hongzhang

Earlier, Timothy Richard had suggested to Li Hongzhang, an important figure in the imperial court, that the government "should commence educational reform by setting apart a million taels [of silver] annually for it." To this suggestion, Li replied "that the Chinese government could not afford so great a sum." When Richard explained that this "was seed-money, which would be returned a hundred-fold," Li asked, "when that would be?" When

Richard answered, "it will take twenty years before you can realize the benefits of modern education," Li simply said, "Ah, we cannot wait as long as that."

Neither Li Hongzhang nor Timothy Richard could have thought that the Boxer Rebellion would lead to the Qing government being forced to pay out large indemnity funds and that indemnities would then be used for the development of Chinese education. This was equivalent to forcing the government to set aside a large sum for investing in education.

The Bible says, there is "a time to plant and a time to harvest" and "those who plant in tears will harvest with shouts of joy."

Just before the formation of the People's Republic of China on July 4, 1949, Vice Chairman of the Central People's Government Liu Shaoqi wrote a report to Joseph Stalin, "Britain and the U.S. alone have established 31 universities and specialized schools, 29 libraries, 324 high schools and 2,364 elementary schools......"

Peking Union Medical College

Chapter 2
University System

Notable Chinese universities founded by missionaries include:

Yenching University, founded by American and British churches in 1919. Its first president was American missionary John Leighton Stuart. Its motto was "Freedom through Truth for Service." Later, its humanities and science departments were integrated into Peking University, while its engineering departments were merged into Tsinghua University. Its campus was where Peking University is located today.

John Leighton Stuart at Yenching University

St. John's University in Shanghai, the first Chinese university to be registered in Washington, D.C. It included departments for the humanities, sciences, medicine, agriculture, and theology; the university motto was "Light and Truth." Later, its departments were merged into Fudan University, East China Normal University, Shanghai Jiaotong University, and others. Its campus was where East China University of Political Science and Law is located today.

Hujiang University, founded by American Baptist missionaries. It established the first sociology department in China and was later merged into East China Normal University. Its campus was where the University of Shanghai for Science and Technology is located today; its motto was "Faith, Righteousness, Diligence, Love."

Ginling College

Ginling College, China's first women's college, founded jointly by multiple American churches. In 1919, its first graduating class had five people. By 1951, when it was merged into Nanjing Normal University, there had been 999 female graduates, often referred to as the 999 roses of China.

Hangchow Christian College, founded by the American Presbyterian Church later merged into Hangzhou University and Zhejiang University. Its campus was where Zhejiang University is located today.

Aurora University was later merged into Fudan University, Shanghai Jiaotong University, Tongji University, and others.

American Methodist Episcopal Church
The University of Nanking
Now Nanjing University

United Presbyterian Church and
British Baptist Missionary Society
Cheeloo University
Now Shandong University

American Methodist Episcopal Church
Central University in China
Now Jiangsu University

United Presbyterian Church
Canton Christian College
Now Zhongshan University

American British and Canadian Churches
West China Union University
Now Sichuan University

US Episcopal Church
Central China University
Now Central China Normal University

American Methodist Episcopal Church
Fukien Christian University
Now Fuzhou University

American Methodist Episcopal Church
Hwa Nan Women's College
Now Fujian Normal University

Catholic Church
Tianjin Normal University
Now Hebei University

Catholic Church
Fu Jen Catholic University
Now Beijing Normal University

Lin Chi-Ping: Many scholars recognize that we need to find the intermediary person to China's modernization. They mediated influences from the West that led to today's modernization. To mediate China's modernization, there are three possible types. The first are soldiers who came to fight. After fighting, they left. The second are business people; after they did their business, earned their money, they also left. Only one kind of people, missionaries. On the one hand, they were very well educated. On the other hand, they delved deeply into the lowest levels of China's society. In this process of mediating modernization, they played very important roles. Some missionaries left their mark on history.

Chinese people should never forget that in this journey from closed and isolated to open and cosmopolitan, from darkness to enlightenment, the messengers of God were the ones that led us in our first step forward.

CHAPTER 3
Cultural Enlightenment

In 1815, British missionary William Milne began printing in Malacca the first monthly periodical written in Chinese, *The Chinese Monthly Magazine.*

In 1823, British missionary Walter Medhurst founded China's first letterpress magazine, *News from All Lands.*

In 1832, American missionary Elijah Coleman Bridgman founded China's first English periodical, *The Chinese Repository*, in Guangzhou.

In 1833, German missionary Karl Gützlaff of Guangzhou founded China's first Chinese periodical, *The Eastern Western Monthly Magazine.*

In 1870, British missionary Timothy Richard came to China and founded the extremely influential Christian Literature Society for China. The Society published a newspaper, *Multinational Communique,* with missionary Young John Allen as editor-in-chief.

Kang Youwei, leader of the Hundred Days' Reform,[10] was an avid reader of *Multinational Communique* and submitted his own work in response to the newspaper's call for articles in 1894. In fact, Kang said: "I owe my conversion to reform chiefly to the writings of two missionaries, Rev. Timothy Richard and Rev. Dr.

Young J. Allen."

Another leader of the Hundred Day's Reform, Liang Qichao, had previously served as Richard's personal secretary. He developed a reading list, "Bibliography of Western Learning," that he recommended to other Chinese. The Christian Literature Society for China was the publisher of 22 items on his list, chief among them Richard's *Essentials of the West's Recent History* and Allen's *Multinational Communique*.

Multinational Communique   *Young John Allen*

Sun Yat-sen, leader of the Xinhai Revolution that overthrew China's last dynasty, entrusted *Multinational Communique* to publish his "A Letter to Li Hongzhang," further demonstrating the strong influence of this newspaper.

---

[10] The Hundred Days of Reform was a failed 103-day national, cultural, political and educational reform movement from 11 June to 21 September 1898 in late Qing Dynasty China. It was undertaken by the young Guangxu Emperor and his reform-minded supporters including Kang Youwei, Liang Qichao and others.

Lin Chi-Ping: I want to discuss one controversial figure in particular — William Martin, who was a missionary in Ningbo for ten years. He understood Chinese culture. He wrote a very famous book, *Evidences of Christianity*, also widely circulated in Japan. In 1858 and then 1860, the Second Opium War occurred, followed by the Treaty of Tien-ching and the Convention of Peking, which included negotiations with the American Minister to China. Martin became the interpreter for the American Minister. That was a huge offense at that time. Later, when we went to do some research, we discovered that through his participation in the negotiation of these treaties, Martin concluded that the Chinese did not understand international law at all.

William Martin

The Chinese would accept the unacceptable and reject what should be accepted during negotiations. For example, extraterritoriality, an extremely important provision that would be a huge affront to national sovereignty, the Chinese accepted very quickly. The Chinese people had long followed a simple rule called the Sino-barbarian dichotomy: barbarians rule over barbarians and the Chinese rule over the Chinese. When the Chinese negotiator agreed, Martin expressed his concern, but to no end. On the other hand, he believed that one of the most important clauses for the Chinese to accept, for example, was the exchange of ambassadors and establishment of diplomatic relations. This provision would have benefited the Chinese, but the Chinese government adamantly refused. Why? Martin explained that the Chinese thought that the barbarians were ugly and would be unsightly if they resided in Beijing and so rejected that proposition.

Martin later studied international law, earning a doctorate in law. He began translating international laws for China. He felt that a lack of Chinese understanding of international law would leave the country at a disadvantage in exchanges with foreigners. Martin was the beginning of Chinese international law. He even translated the influential book *Elements of International Law* into Chinese.

The School of Combined Learning

Martin believed that the Chinese needed to improve their education system so their own people could understand foreign languages, communicate with foreigners, and could improve understanding on both sides. The late Qing Dynasty established the School of Combined Learning to train the Chinese with talent in languages. Martin also spent a great deal of effort hiring teachers with varied expertise, including in the fields of technology, chemistry, and medicine. When it opened up admissions, no one applied because China's Imperial Examination did not test these subjects. Martin began his opposition to the Imperial Examination as part of the reforms to save China. The reformers Liang Qichao and Kang Youwei were very close with Martin. Later during the reform, they removed the Imperial Examination, an important step in the modernization of China. Martin played an important role behind the scenes.

Chapter 4
China's World Stage

The missionaries not only had a profound impact within China, but they also helped bring China onto the world stage.

In the early 19th century, Robert Morrison established the first Chinese class in England.

Scottish missionary James Legge was the first to systematically research classical Chinese texts. From 1861 to 1886, he spent 25 years translating 28 volumes of Chinese classics, including the *Four Books* and *Five Classics*, into English.

Lin Chi-Ping: His ability was amazing. He translated the

James Legge and his chinese assistants

entirety of China's *Thirteen Confucian Classics* into English. Nowadays, we can't even name the thirteen classics. He translated all thirteen and added explanatory notes and commentary. I've read his books. After his translation, for example, of Mencius, there are many pages of commentary and remarks made by generations of scholars. Legge's books leave a remarkable impression. After he retired, he returned to Oxford and founded the Department of Chinese Studies and thus became the earliest great Sinologist.

James Legge's student, William Soothill, was a missionary in Wenzhou, China for 25 years. He served as President of Shanxi University. After his retirement, he returned to Oxford University as a professor. He was the first to translate the *Analects* of Confucius to modern English.

Lin Chi-Ping: This was a series: William Soothill was James Legge's student. Then, after Soothill retired, he became a professor and educated the most famous student of that time: John King Fairbank of Harvard University. Missionaries played an extremely important role for Sinology, evident in all present-day Chinese Studies in Europe and the U.S.

Pearl Buck, a daughter of missionaries who grew up in rural China, author of *The Good Earth* trilogy, painted a rich picture of Chinese customs and peasant life. For her work, she became the first American woman to win the Nobel Prize for Literature.

Pearl Buck

Chapter 5
Opium Ban

In the 19th century, opium usage was spreading through China like cancer.

The missionaries universally condemned the opium trade. The first medical missionary, Peter Parker, wrote a letter to the Imperial Commissioner, Lin Zexu in 1840, describing opium as a worrisome evil.

The American missionary William Martin published a primer in 1856, analyzing the ethical and legal issues of opium.

Sinologist James Legge warned the British government: "Cease to do evil, and learn to do well."

Hudson Taylor said: "I am profoundly convinced that the opium traffic is doing more evil in China in a week than Missions are doing good in a year."

In 1874, missionaries formed The Anglo-Oriental Society for the Suppression of the Opium Trade, whose primary function was lobbying the British Government to cease its involvement in the opium trade.

In 1906, Hampden DuBose circulated a petition signed by over 1,000 missionaries in China to present to the Emperor, as well as British and American governments. They received the support of the American Congress and the International Opium Commission.

It was under the strong influence of missionaries that the Treaty of Wanghia between China and the U.S. declared the opium trade as illegal.

The missionaries pressured their own governments to prohibit the opium trade while helping addicts rehabilitate. In 1871, these missionaries established the first rehabilitation center in Hangzhou. By the early 20th century, there were more than 100 such centers across the country.

Xi Shengmo

British missionary David Hill helped a Confucian scholar in Shanxi named Xi Zizhi conquer his opium addiction. In response, Xi took on a new name, Xi Shengmo, meaning Conqueror of Demons, and established rehabilitation centers called "Heavenly Invitation Offices" that ultimately helped countless other individuals conquer their own addictions. He left behind a beautiful legacy.

Chapter 6
Modern Sports

One hundred fifty years ago, the Western powers ridiculed the Chinese as sick men of Asia while the Western missionaries delivered the spirit of sport.

In 1876, the Young Men's Christian Association (YMCA) entered China, introducing and promoting modern sports, including basketball, volleyball, soccer, ping pong, tennis, baseball, track and field, swimming, diving, and gymnastics, etc.

Eric Liddell

In 1925, Olympic gold medalist Eric Liddell came to Tianjin from Britain to help build the world-class Minyuan Stadium in Tianjin. The Stadium attracted multiple international competitions.

In 1932, the one who pushed China to start participating in the Olympic Games was the Secretary of the YMCA's National Committee, Wang Zhengting.

Wang Zhengting

Chapter 7
Women's Freedom

The painful practice of foot binding had plagued Chinese women since antiquity. In 1874, British missionary John MacGowan began China's first anti-foot binding society in Xiamen. Over 1,000 women signed a pledge to abandon the practice.

Women with bound feet

In 1895, Mary Richard and others founded the Natural Foot Society in Shanghai, distributing pamphlets and organizing meetings calling for women to return to their natural state.

Helping a Chinese woman to unbind her feet

The teachers and students in church schools and other women who read the Bible led the cultural reform; not a single one of them bound their feet.

Missionary Young John Allen also spoke out, arguing that the strengthening of China could not be achieved without the liberation of Chinese women.

Chinese philosopher Hu Shih reflected: "Suddenly some missionaries came from the West. In addition to preaching, they also brought a few new customs, some new perspectives, many new lessons, and among those, the biggest is teaching us to view women also as human beings."

The right for women to be educated was not officially

recognized by the Qing government until 1907. But as early as in 1844, missionary Mary Ann Aldersey founded China's first school for girls in Ningbo.

Mary Ann Aldersey

In 1850, missionary Eliza Bridgman established the Bridgman Memorial School for Girls in Shanghai, today's Shanghai Ninth Secondary School. Among the students to pass through Bridgman Memorial was Ni Guizhen, a rarity among women of her time, with her large, unbound feet. She was a descendent of the eminent Ming dynasty scholar and Christian, Xu Guangqi. Ni Guizhen later had three daughters who would turn out to be among the most significant political figures of their time. They were Song Ailing, Song Qingling, and Song Meiling. The father to the Song Sisters was Charlie Song, who was originally a pastor.

In 1905, missionaries founded China's first women's college in Beijing, the North China Union Women's College. They would later go on to found Hwa Nan College, Ginling College for Women, and others, training for China its earliest set of female college graduates, including the famous writer Bing Xin and others.

In his book, *The Awakening of China*, the missionary William Martin foresaw: "In years to come, the education of Chinese youth will begin at the mother's knee." His prediction has long been fulfilled by countless Chinese mothers.

Ni Guizhen with her three daughters Song Ailing, Song Qingling and Song Meiling

Chapter 8
Charity and Relief

During a series of persecutions in the third century AD, Roman officers ordered St. Lawrence to turn over the treasures of the church. St. Lawrence brought forward the poor, the disabled, and the sick, saying: "This is the Church's treasure." The Romans roasted him to death on a gridiron.

Today in Florida, there is still a homeless shelter named after St. Lawrence.

Jesus once said: "Whatever you did for one of the least of these brothers and sisters of mine, you did for me."

China's first orphanage was founded in the late 1840s by the Berlin Missionary Society in Hong Kong. By 1914, there were 37 orphanages established by churches, taking care of around 2,500 orphans.

China's first school for the blind was established in 1874 by the missionary William Murray in Beijing. Murray also designed a Braille system for Chinese.

China's first school for the deaf was established in 1898 by Annette Mills in Yantai. By 1936, there were over a dozen across the country.

China's first mental hospital was established by medical missionary John Kerr in Guangzhou, named Canton Refuge for the Insane.

China's first leper hospital was founded in 1892 by David Duncan Main in Hangzhou, named The Hospital of Universal Benevolence. In 1940, there were 51 leper hospitals in China, of which 40 were associated with the church.

Timothy Richard

Timothy Richard made an enormous impact on charity in China. He established five orphanages, each of which took in 100 children and subsequently trained them to be skilled workers.

During the Northern Chinese Famine in 1877, Richard saved over 70,000 individuals and established seven schools for famine orphans.

Richard said that a truly loving heart is much greater than empty theology.

The Chinese people will not forget that during the Nanking Massacre, the American missionary at Ginling College, Wilhelmina Minnie Vautrin, transformed the college into a refugee camp and protected around 10,000 women and children. Another American missionary, Miner Bates, was one of the leaders of the International Committee of the Nanking Safety Zone, which helped protect over 200,000 refugees.

Wilhelmina Minnie Vautrin

China's first school for the blind

David Hill and lepers

Chapter 9
Medicine and Healthcare

Richard once asked a Chinese gentleman what he thought of the New Testament. After pondering for a few seconds, he replied: "Perhaps the most wonderful thought was this – that man might become the temple of the Holy Ghost."

Beginning with Jesus, originating from the same love, the saving of the soul and the healing of the body always came hand in hand.

As early as 1565, Catholic bishop Melchior Carneiro built a hospital in Macau, treating all patients, regardless of whether they were part of the church.

After Morrison arrived in China, in 1820, he invited Dr. John Livingstone to open a clinic in Macau.

In 1835, American medical missionary Peter Parker opened the Ophthalmic Hospital in Guangzhou, complete with separate areas for reception, diagnosis, dispensary, operation, post-operation observation, and a waiting room large enough for 200 people. In 1842, it developed into a comprehensive hospital, the Canton Pok Tsai Hospital. Sun Yat-Sen was an intern at this hospital.

In 1838, British missionary William Lockhart founded the first western hospital in Shanghai, precursor to today's Renji Hospital, where all patients were treated free of charge. He recalled: "Crowds of people daily came to the hospital, urgently, often boisterously, requesting to be attended."

There was a missionary named Deborah Douw who was commissioned by the American Presbyterian Church to go to Beijing. At the time, women in China suffered greatly from the pains of childbirth. When children were born, midwives would often simply pull out a splint from a bamboo mat to cut the umbilical cord and sprinkle some dust to stop the bleeding. Many children would die within days.

Seeing all of this firsthand, Douw wept. She subsequently returned to the U.S. and spent eight years raising funds from various churches. In 1885, she returned to Beijing, built 12 bungalows, and thus founded China's first women's hospital, Douw Hospital, today's Beijing Municipal No. 6 Hospital.

Douw hospital

Later, Douw brought in departments in addition to obstetrics and gynecology and established many hospitals in other parts of China.

Church hospital

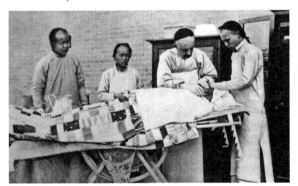

Medical missionary

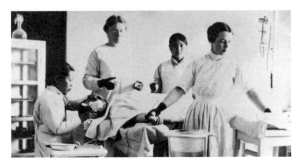

Operation room

According to surveys from 1920, there were a total of 820 hospitals and clinics established by missionaries in China.

Renowned hospitals in China established by missionaries include:
Peking Union Medical College Hospital
Tongji Hospital
West China Hospital
Qilu Hospital of Shandong University
Renji Hospital
Canton Pok Tsai Hospital
Tongren Hospital
Pu Ren Hospital
Tsingchow Guangde Hospital
Soochow Hospital
Yali Hospital
Hangzhou Guangji Hospital
Mackenzie Hospital
Yong Chun Hospital
Mackay Memorial Hospital

The driving force behind the sacrificial service of these missionaries was the love embodied by Jesus on the cross. From the establishment of the first hospital to each subsequent building, they would hang a cross at the door.

Today, the Chinese people have long been accustomed to seeing the symbol of the cross on hospitals, and many people think of the International Red Cross.

But actually, the representation of hospitals with the symbol of a cross is unique to China. Hospitals in the U.S. do not have crosses; hospitals in Europe do not have crosses; and we do not see hospitals in India with crosses either. Nevertheless, in China, every hospital has a cross. This is because all the early hospitals in China were built by missionaries.

Cross on hospital buildings in China

After 1949, despite the changing times, throughout China, whether it may be urban or rural, atop hospitals and clinics, the cross has remained. How could we not consider this a miracle, a sign of grace!

Reflections of Computer Engineers in the U.S. Silicon Valley:

For thousands of years, China has been in God's plan. God never forgets China.

So many people, so long ago, started caring for this land.

They are totally different from the imperialists. They came to help China. They led China to the bigger world. They brought the Gospel to the Chinese.

Truly! God's love brought them to China. Think of ourselves. We are just the opposite. We came to America from China for a better life. Such a contrast!

People help those they know. They help friends. Missionaries did not know us. But they came across the ocean to help us and lift us from poverty. Such selfless love! Where does it come from? From God. God said, love others as yourself. Such profound love!

God even remembers lepers and mental patients. He sent His servants to love them. God's love is so great and far reaching!

So many of God's messengers give their lives to this land. Wherever God's love touches, wherever God's spirit descends, life is transformed. A nation is revived. Because God creates life, being with Him means life, means vitality, means civilization.

Pastor Thomas Wang, founder of Great Commission Center International: My family believed in Jesus starting from my grandmother who was led by a missionary. My parents lived in Baoding. They attended a missionary school there. My elder sister worked in Beijing Union Hospital. My younger sister studied in Cheeloo University in Jinan. My youngest sister attended Yenching University. My brother was also a student there.

I was born in Douw Hospital in Beijing. Douw Hospital was a hospital built by missionaries. My middle school was built by missionaries, Beijing Soongsil Middle School. Later, I attended colleges. First, Fu Jen University, a Catholic college. Next, St. John's University, a Christian college.

Oh, we are truly thankful! How? God sent so many Western

missionaries, leaving their hometowns, enduring so much hardship and pain, to come and be with us. Many died in China. Their tombs still remain there. They came from thousands of miles away, and brought such a great love to us!

Today we ask ourselves: Do we have the same great love for our own countrymen? We feel this responsibility.

God, give us grace! Have mercy on Chinese Christians and churches. I believe that, very quickly, we will see Chinese missionaries go all over the world to spread the Good News. This will happen by the grace of God. This is the conviction in my heart.

105 people were baptized on November 3rd, 1904

One day, when the origin and meaning of these crosses becomes universally recognized, they will shine an even brighter light and bring forth an even greater love.

There is a Chinese proverb: "When drinking water, one should never forget those who dug the well." Today, we should not forget the missionaries who painstakingly dug the first wells for each and every aspect of China's modernization.

Nor should we forget the one who guided them to go to China, to sacrifice their lives for China, to bring prosperity to China, all through the light of heaven, the love of the cross.

All praise be to God!

THEME SONG
In the Same World

Canaan Hymns #76
Lyric and music by Xiao Min

In the same world,
Below the same sky,
Under the same sun,
The moon and the stars
Sharing the same space.

The revolving world,
Filled with God's grace.
We sing together,
God's love fills the world.

The love of the Cross,
Breaking the barriers of
Different skin colors and languages.
Everywhere, God's children
Are closely connected.

Ah, the Cross!
Your love is most complete,
Your love is most beautiful,
Until forever.

NESTORIAN TABLET

Nestorian Tablet

Eulogizing the Propagation of the Illustrious Religion in China
with a Preface, composed by a priest of the Syriac Church, 781 A.D.

Horne Introduction:

This remarkable record of the fact that Christianity flourished in medieval China is a huge stone about ten feet high. Carven dragons and a cross adorn its summit, and its main shaft is completely covered with some two thousand Chinese characters. It stands now in the Peilin or "Forest of Tablets" in Sian-fu, this Peilin being a great hall specially devoted to the preservation of old historic tablets. Up to a few years ago the ancient stone stood with other unvalued monuments in the grounds of a Buddhist monastery, exposed to all the assaults of the elements. Only European urging has led to its being preserved in the Peilin.

The Nestorian sect of Christians still exists in Western Asia and was in a thriving condition in Syria in the sixth century. It sent missionaries widely over Asia. Marco Polo recorded having found Christian churches in China; and Roman Catholic missionaries of later centuries found there a few Nestorians still practising a debased form of their half-forgotten faith. This much concerning the Nestorian Christianity in China we have long known. Then, with the modern opening of the empire, the old Nestorian stone was found. It tells its own history, and tells it plainly, how the Nestorian monks came, how Chinese officials were appointed to listen to their explanations, and gravely approved of the new religion as having "excellent principles." Various emperors accepted, or at least included, Christianity among their religions; and the faith prospered, and had many thousands of followers, and in the year A.D. 781 erected this stone in commemoration of its triumphs.

Now, alas, only the stone remains. The record of the sect's decay has needed no stone to make it manifest. Nestorian Christianity, shut off from its mother land by the rise of the Mohammedan powers in between, proved unable to resist the inroads of ignorance and superstition and changing political affairs. It degenerated and disappeared.

"Behold the unchangeably true and invisible, who existed through all eternity without origin; the far-seeing perfect intelligence, whose mysterious existence is everlasting; operating on primordial substance he created the universe, being more excellent than all holy intelligences, inasmuch as he is the source of all that is honorable. This is our eternal true lord God, triune and mysterious in substance. He appointed the cross as the means for determining the four cardinal points, he moved the original spirit, and produced the two principles of nature; the somber void was changed, and heaven and earth were opened out; the sun and moon revolved, and day and night commenced; having perfected all inferior objects, he then made the first man; upon him he bestowed an excellent disposition, giving him in charge the government of all created beings; man, acting out the original principles of his nature, was pure and unostentatious; his unsullied and expansite mind was free from the least inordinate desire; until Satan introduced the seeds of falsehood, to deteriorate his purity of principle; the opening thus commenced in his virtue gradually enlarged, and by this crevice in his nature was obscured and rendered vicious; hence three hundred and sixty-five sects followed each other in continuous track, inventing every species of doctrinal complexity; while some pointed to material objects as the source of their faith, others reduced all to vacancy, even to the annihilation of the two primeval principles, some sought to call down blessings by prayers and supplications, while others by an assumption of excellence held themselves up as superior to their fellows; their intellects and thoughts continually wavering, their minds and affections incessantly on the move, they never obtained their vast desires, but being exhausted and distressed they revolved in their own heated atmosphere; till by an accumulation of obscurity they lost their path, and after long groping in darkness they were unable to return. Thereupon, our Trinity being divided in nature, the illustrious and honorable Messiah, veiling his true dignity, appeared in the world as a man; angelic powers promulgated the glad tidings, a virgin gave birth to the Holy One in Syria; a bright star announced the felicitous event, and Persians observing the splendor came to present tribute; the ancient dispensation, as declared by the twenty-four holy men [the writers of the Old Testament], was then fulfilled, and he laid down great principles for the government of families and kingdoms; he established the new religion of the silent operation of the pure spirit of the Triune; he rendered virtue subservient to direct faith; he fixed the extent of the eight boundaries, thus completing the truth and freeing it from dross; he opened the gate of the three constant principles, introducing life and destroying death; he suspended the bright sun to invade the chambers of darkness, and the falsehoods of the devil were thereupon defeated; he set in motion the vessel of mercy by which to ascend to the bright mansions, whereupon rational beings were then released, having thus completed the manifestation of his power, in clear day he ascended to his true station.

Twenty-seven sacred books [the number in the New Testament] have been left, which disseminate intelligence by unfolding the original transforming principles. By the rule for admission, it is the custom to apply the water of baptism, to wash away all superficial show and to cleanse and purify the neophytes. As a seal, they hold the cross, whose influence is reflected in every direction, uniting all without distinction. As they strike the wood, the fame of their benevolence is diffused abroad; worshiping toward the east, they hasten on the way to life and glory; they preserve the beard to symbolize their outward actions, they shave the crown to indicate the absence of inward affections; they do not keep slaves, but put noble and mean all on an equality; they do not amass wealth, but cast all their property into the common stock; they fast, in order to perfect themselves by self-inspection; they submit to restraints, in order to strengthen themselves by silent watchfulness; seven times a day they have worship and praise for the benefit of the living and the dead; once in seven days they sacrifice, to cleanse the heart and return to purity.

It is difficult to find a name to express the excellence of the true and unchangeable doctrine; but as its meritorious operations are manifestly displayed, by accommodation it is named the Illustrious Religion. Now without holy men, principles cannot become expanded; without principles, holy men cannot become magnified; but with holy men and right principles, united as the two parts of a signet, the world becomes civilized and enlightened.

In the time of the accomplished Emperor Tai-tsung, the illustrious and magnificent founder of the dynasty, among the enlightened and holy men who arrived was the most-virtuous Olopun, from the country of Syria. Observing the azure clouds, he bore the true sacred books; beholding the direction of the winds, he braved difficulties and dangers. In the year of our Lord 635 he arrived at Chang-an; the Emperor sent his Prime Minister, Duke Fang Hiuen-ling; who, carrying the official staff to the west border, conducted his guest into the interior; the sacred books were translated in the imperial library, the sovereign investigated the subject in his private apartments; when becoming deeply impressed with the rectitude and truth of the religion, he gave special orders for its dissemination.

In the seventh month of the year A.D. 638 the following imperial proclamation was issued:

"Right principles have no invariable name, holy men have no invariable station; instruction is established in accordance with the locality, with the object of benefiting the people at large. The greatly virtuous Olopun, of the kingdom of Syria, has brought his sacred books and images from that distant part, and has presented them at our chief capital. Having examined the principles of this religion, we find them to be purely excellent and natural; investigating its originating source, we find it has taken its rise from the establishment of important truths; its ritual is free from perplexing expressions, its principles will survive when the framework is forgot; it is beneficial to all creatures; it is advantageous to mankind. Let it be published throughout the Empire, and let the proper authority build a Syrian church in the capital in the I-ning May, which shall be governed by twenty-one priests. When the virtue of the Chau Dynasty declined, the rider on the azure ox ascended to the west; the principles of the great Tang becoming resplendent, the Illustrious breezes have come to fan the East."

Orders were then issued to the authorities to have a true portrait of the Emperor taken; when it was transferred to the wall of the church, the dazzling splendor of the celestial visage irradiated the Illustrious portals. The sacred traces emitted a felicitous influence, and shed a perpetual splendor over the holy precincts. According to the Illustrated Memoir of the Western Regions, and the historical books of the Han and Wei dynasties, the kingdom of Syria reaches south to the Coral Sea; on the north it joins the Gem Mountains; on the west it extends toward the borders of the immortals and the flowery forests; on the east it lies open to the violent winds and tideless waters. The country produces fire-proof cloth, life-restoring incense, bright moon-pearls, and night-luster gems. Brigands and robbers are unknown, but the people enjoy happiness and peace. None but Illustrious laws prevail; none but the virtuous are raised to sovereign power. The land is broad and ample, and its literary productions are perspicuous and clear.

The Emperor Kau-tsung respectfully succeeded his ancestor, and was still more beneficent toward the institution of truth. In every province he caused Illustrious churches to be erected, and ratified the honor conferred upon Olopun, making him the great conservator of doctrine for the preservation of the State. While this doctrine pervaded every channel, the State became enriched and tranquility abounded. Every city was full of churches, and the royal family enjoyed luster and happiness. In the year A.D. 699 the Buddhists, gaining power, raised their voices in the eastern metropolis; in the year A.D. 713, some low fellows excited ridicule and spread slanders in the western capital. At that time there was the chief priest Lohan, the greatly virtuous Kie-leih, and others of noble estate from the golden regions, lofty-minded priests, having abandoned all worldly interests; who unitedly maintained the grand principles and preserved them entire to the end. The high-principled Emperor Hiuen-tsung caused the Prince of Ning and others, five princes in all, personally to visit the felicitous edifice; he established the place of worship; he restored the consecrated timbers which had been temporarily thrown down; and re-erected the sacred stones which for a time had been desecrated.

In A.D. 742 orders were given to the great general Kau Lih-sz', to send the five sacred portraits and have them placed in the church, and a gift of a hundred pieces of silk accompanied these pictures of intelligence. Although the dragon's beard was then remote, their bows and swords were still within reach; while the solar horns sent forth their rays, and celestial visages seemed close at hand. In A.D. 744 the priest Kih-ho, in the kingdom of Syria, looking toward the star [of China], was attracted by its transforming influence, and observing the sun [*i.e.*, the Emperor], came to pay court to the most honorable. The Emperor commanded the priest Lo-han, the priest Pu-lun, and others, seven in all, together with the greatly virtuous Kih-ho, to perform a service of merit in the Hing-king palace. Thereupon the Emperor composed mottoes for the sides of the church, and the tablets were graced with the royal inscriptions; the accumulated gems emitted their effulgence, while their sparkling brightness vied with the ruby clouds; the transcripts of intelligence suspended in the void shot forth their rays as reflected by the sun; the bountiful gifts exceeded the height of the southern hills; the bedewing favors were deep as the eastern sea. Nothing is beyond the range of the right principle, and what is permissible may be identified; nothing is beyond the power of the holy man, and that which is practicable may be related.

The accomplished and enlightened Emperor Suh-tsung rebuilt the Illustrious churches in Ling-wu and four other places; great benefits were conferred, and felicity began to increase; great munificence was displayed, and the imperial State became established. The accomplished and military Emperor Tai-tsung magnified the sacred succession, and honored the latent principle of nature; always, on the incarnation-day, he bestowed celestial incense, and ordered the performance of a service of merit; he distributed of the imperial viands, in order to shed a glory on the Illustrious Congregation. Heaven is munificent in the dissemination of blessings, whereby the benefits of life are extended; the holy man embodies the original principle of virtue, whence he is able to counteract noxious influences.

Our sacred and sage-like, accomplished and military Emperor Kien-chung appointed the eight branches of government, according to which he advanced or degraded the intelligent and dull; he opened up the nine categories, by means of which he renovated the Illustrious decrees; his transforming influence pervaded the most abstruse principles, while openness of heart distinguished his devotions. Thus, by correct and enlarged purity of principle, and undeviating consistency in sympathy with others; by extended commiseration rescuing multitudes from misery, while disseminating blessings on all around, the cultivation of our doctrine gained a grand basis, and by gradual advances its influence was diffused. If the winds and rains are seasonable, the world will be at rest; men will be guided by principle, inferior objects will be pure; the living will be at ease, and the dead will rejoice; the thoughts will produce their appropriate response, the affections will be free, and the eyes will be sincere; such is the laudable condition which we of the Illustrious Religion are laboring to attain.

Our great benefactor, the Imperially conferred purple-gown priest, I-sz', titular Great Statesman of the Banqueting-house, Associated Secondary Military Commissioner for the Northern Region, and Examination-palace Overseer, was naturally mild and graciously disposed; his mind susceptible of sound doctrine, he was diligent in the performance; from the distant city of Rajagriha, he came to visit China; his principles more lofty than those of the three dynasties, his practise was perfect in every department; at first he applied himself to duties pertaining to the palace, eventually his name was inscribed on the military roll. When the Duke Koh Tsz'-i, Secondary Minister of State and Prince of Fan-yang, at first conducted the military in the northern region, the Emperor Suh-tsung made him (I-sz') his attendant on his travels; although he was a private chamberlain, he assumed no distinction on the march; he was as claws and teeth to the duke, and in rousing the military he was as ears and eyes; he distributed the wealth conferred upon him, not accumulating treasure for his private use; he made offerings of the jewelry which had been given by imperial favor, he spread out a golden carpet for devotion; now he repaired the old churches, anon he increased the number of religious establishments; he honored and decorated the various edifices, till they resembled the plumage of the pheasant in its flight; moreover, practising the discipline of the Illustrious Religion, he distributed his riches in deeds of benevolence; every year he assembled those in the sacred office from four churches, and respectfully engaged them for fifty days in purification and preparation; the naked came and were clothed; the sick were attended to and restored; the dead were buried in repose; even among the most pure and self-denying of the Buddhists, such excellence was never heard of; the white-clad members of the Illustrious Congregation, now considering these men, have desired to engrave a broad tablet, in order to set forth a eulogy of their magnanimous deeds.

ODE
The true Lord is without origin,
Profound, invisible, and unchangeable;
With power and capacity to perfect and transform,
He raised up the earth and established the heavens.
Divided in nature, he entered the world,
To save and to help without bounds;
The sun arose, and darkness was dispelled,

All bearing witness to his true original.
The glorious and resplendent, accomplished Emperor,
Whose principles embraced those of preceding monarchs,
Taking advantage of the occasion, suppressed turbulence;
Heaven was spread out and the earth was enlarged.
When the pure, bright Illustrious Religion
Was introduced to our Tang Dynasty,
The Scriptures were translated, and churches built,
And the vessel set in motion for the living and the dead;
Every kind of blessing was then obtained,
And all the kingdoms enjoyed a state of peace.
When Kau-tsung succeeded to his ancestral estate,
He rebuilt the edifices of purity;
Palaces of concord, large and light,
Covered the length and breadth of the land.
The true doctrine was clearly announced,
Overseers of the church were appointed in due form;
The people enjoyed happiness and peace,
While all creatures were exempt from calamity and distress.
When Hiuen-tsung commenced his sacred career,
He applied himself to the cultivation of truth and rectitude;
His imperial tablets shot forth their effulgence,
And the celestial writings mutually reflected their splendors.
The imperial domain was rich and luxuriant,
While the whole land rendered exalted homage;
Every business was flourishing throughout,
And the people all enjoyed prosperity.
Then came Suh-tsung, who commenced anew,
And celestial dignity marked the Imperial movements.
Sacred as the moon's unsullied expanse,
While felicity was wafted like nocturnal gales.
Happiness reverted to the Imperial household,
The autumnal influences were long removed;
Ebullitions were allayed, and risings suppressed,
And thus our dynasty was firmly built up.

Tai-tsung the filial and just
Combined in virtue with heaven and earth;
By his liberal bequests the living were satisfied,
And property formed the channel of imparting succor.
By fragrant mementoes he rewarded the meritorious,
With benevolence he dispensed his donations;
The solar concave appeared in dignity,
And the lunar retreat was decorated to extreme.
When Kien-chung succeeded to the throne,
He began the cultivation of intelligent virtue;
His military vigilance extended to the four seas,
And his accomplished purity influenced all lands.
His light penetrated the secrecies of men,
And to him the diversities of objects were seen as in a mirror;
He shed a vivifying influence through the whole realm of nature,
And all outer nations took him for example.
The true doctrine, how expansive!
Its responses are minute;
How difficult to name it!
To elucidate the three in one.
The sovereign has the power to act!
While the ministers record;
We raise this noble monument!
To the praise of great felicity.

This was erected in the 2nd year of Kien-chung, of the Tang Dynasty [A.D. 781], on the 7th day of the 1st month, being Sunday.

Written by Lu Siu-yen, Secretary to Council, formerly Military Superintendent for Tai-chau; while the Bishop Ning-shu had the charge of the congregations of the Illustrious in the East.

[The following is written in Syriac, running down the right and left sides of the Chinese inscription above.]
"Adam, Deacon, Vicar-episcopal and Pope of China. In the time of

the Father of Fathers, the Lord John Joshua, the Universal Patriarch."

[The following is in Syriac at the foot of the stone.]
"In the year of the Greeks one thousand and ninety-two, the Lord Jazedbuzid, Priest and Vicar-episcopal of Cumdan the royal city, son of the enlightened Mailas, Priest of Balkh a city of Turkestan, set up this tablet, whereon is inscribed the Dispensation of our Redeemer, and the preaching of the apostolic missionaries to the King of China."

[After this, in Chinese characters, follows:]
"The Priest Lingpau."

[Then follows in Syriac:]
"Adam the Deacon, son of Jazedbuzid, Vicar-episcopal.
The Lord Sergius, Priest and Vicar-episcopal.
Sabar Jesus, Priest.
Gabriel, Priest, Archdeacon, and Ecclesiarch of Cumdan and Sarag."

[The following subscription is appended in Chinese:]
"Assistant Examiner: the High Statesman of the Sacred rites, the Imperially conferred purple-gown Chief Presbyter and Priest Yi-li."

[On the left-hand edge are the Syriac names of sixty-seven priests, and sixty-one are given in Chinese.]

Source:

Charles F. Horne, ed., *The Sacred Books and Early Literature of the East*, (New York: Parke, Austin, & Lipscomb, 1917), Vol. XII, *Medieval China*, pp. 381-392.
Scanned by Jerome S. Arkenberg, Cal. State Fullerton.
The text has been modernized by Prof. Arkenberg.

Sources

University of Yale
Divinity School Library Special Collection
Beinecke Library Special Collection

University of London
School of Oriental and African Studies (SOAS)

University of Cambridge
Cambridge Bible Society Library

University of Oxford
Angus Library, Regent's Park College

University of Oxford
Bodleian Library Chinese Collections

Harvard University
Harvard-Yenching Library

University of San Francisco
Ricci Institute for Chinese-Western Cultural History

The Library of the Society of Friends

Library of Congress

Vatican Library